Michael Lieber

Street Life
Afro-American Culture
in Urban Trinidad

Schenkman Publishing Co., Cambridge, Massachusetts

Copyright © 1981 by Schenkman Publishing Company, Inc.

Library of Congress Cataloging in Publication Data

Lieber, Michael, 1945-
  Street Life,

  Bibliography: p.
  1. Trinidad—Social conditions. 2. Social classes
—Trinidad. 3. City and town life—Trinidad.
4. Ethnology—Trinidad. I. Title. II. Title: Afro-
American culture in urban Trinidad.
HN246.A8L53   972.98′304   80-24761
ISBN 0-8161-9033-X
ISBN 0-87073-874-4 (Schenkman : pbk.)

This publication is printed on permanent/durable acid-free paper
MANUFACTURED IN THE UNITED STATES OF AMERICA

to the memory of
Malcolm X

Contents

Introduction

This account—a study of the everyday lives of Afro-American men in a Caribbean city—takes an anthropological approach. Pivotal to such an approach are a method and an outlook. The method, or style of distilling information, is ethnographic; the outlook, or style of assessing observations, is naturalistic.

An ethnographic approach implies that in order to understand the shape of other people's lives, the onlooker must patiently dirty his feet in those people's social terrains for a substantial stretch of time. In contrast to what have become, in my view, overly facile and formalized methods of data collection that quantize and pulverize social life into conveniently assortable "facts", ethnography as a style of work or an analytical stance derives from the belief that the lifeways of a people are an interconnected webbing of outlooks and activities that are best illuminated by careful observation of concrete terrains of social action. The aim is to illuminate the *shape* of what actually goes on, not to seek indices which shed light only indirectly on that shape. Described this way, ethnography may seem a subjective style of work, but its assumptions in fact eschew subjectivism. Precisely because the ethnographer views "life as it is really lived," and not as various models or representations, one goes after life, and not variously conceived indices of it. From an ethnographic point of view, then, *appearances* become paramount. Culture's phenotypic representations are not produced by any genotype, but by the collections of moments and events which make up human experience. Ethnography aims to distill the shape of those styles that emerge out of specific human experiences. This book focuses on one broad range of experience: the transport of Africans to the New World via slavery and the eventual consequences of that involuntary immigration.

History thus becomes the basic fact of life: ways of life unfold historically and biographically, and we must understand such unfoldings if we are to comprehend the "here and now" of ethnographic interest. Structuralism, which has unfortunately come to dominate so much of social inquiry, minimizes surface appearance and history; its adherents prefer instead to create models of various "systems" and "structures" while revealing very little about how life is actually conducted.

An ethnographer with a naturalistic outlook takes the world as it is and seeks to understand its contours by noting how its topography unfolds. He does not extract information from this world through calculated data collection and processing methods; he does not seek to replicate this world in some experimental fashion; he does not transform it into abstract models, and then imagine that such models amount to a skeletal substructure of what is alive and concrete. While the penetrating power of the analytical mind has been so rewarding for the natural sciences, it has been far less productive for the social sciences, as Thomas Kuhn so persuasively argued in his *Structure of Scientific Revolutions.* And while much of nature may be said to be rule-bound, man's activity, a small and special part of nature, is largely history-bound. Nature has its secrets, and man is equipped to discover many of these; but social life has no secrets, merely shapes. Consequently the scientific aim is not discovery, but illumination.

Still, the paramount importance of history as the creator of distinctiveness does not imply that experience is without its universals. Blake urged us to look for the universe in a grain of sand. Each grain of sand has a unique form according to how it has been tumbled, but each one also reflects in its contours basic principles of physical order and thus confirms the overall shape of physical reality. While human experience is variously shaped by the vagaries of history, it still remains essentially *human.* We look for specifics, but every specific activity also points to what is human in essence. Some theorists seem to refute this, claiming that "culture makes man", that we enter life as empty vessels to be filled with the specific contents of our experience. This too is a limited viewpoint. Instead, culture may be regarded as the juncture of history and human nature, such "nature" pointing to the pan-specific features of the species and its various populations. Much intellectual effort has been wasted in the radical polarization of "cultural-historical" from "natural-universal" points of view—hence the acrimony of much of the sociobiology debate. All man's experience is part of his biology; we are never outside of history or outside of biology. The historicity of human experience is a facet of the special quality of man's biology, his style of adaptation. But the task of identifying what universals are appropriate for a biologically-attuned anthropology still remains. Here I think genetics is the wrong place to look. A better place to search is the meeting ground of human dispositions and ecological constraints, the domain so marvelously explored by Gregory Bateson. Ethnography should provide a hint. It is all about learning how and what others learn and how the ethnographer learns about others. Learning projects intrinsic biological capacities onto parochial and universal ranges of experience, yielding culturally specific knowledge always constrained by the limits of the mind and of the world (Bateson 1972).

If there were no "human nature," no recognizable universal human qualities and experiences, then the task of ethnography would be impossible.

Anthropologists have wandered nearly everywhere encountering the limits of human exotica, and yet, for all their disclaimers about the difficulties of intercultural translatability, they have been able to penetrate the activities of strangers in very strange lands. The ability to accomplish this has as much to do with the intuitive rapport which enables any attuned person to comprehend another, as it does with the more formal techniques and methods of cultural analysis. If we rid ourselves of excessively parochial viewpoints we can recognize in others of our species, no matter how exotic and different from ourselves they may seem, human universals on display.

Ethnography cannot simply apply rigorous technique to a world perceived as a collection of facts. This is why the very best ethnographers are those who, in addition to having mastered the formal skills of their trade, exhibit a "feel" for clarifying initially opaque systems of meaning and activity, their own humanity drawn to the humanity of others. Wisdom is rarely invoked in assessing the competence of ethnographic work and the confidence of practitioners. But I, for one, always come away from reading an ethnographic account with some sense of the wisdom—or "human-sense"— of the ethnographer. Experience scanned with a thoughtful eye is the source of wisdom. The really great ethnographers develop this thoughtful eye partly because they know that their experience during fieldwork is not of "systems" or "models" or "structures," but of the linked biographies of human beings like themselves.

"Culture" has been and continues to be the keyword of anthropology. Whatever the different dispositions and orientations of anthropologists, they have nearly all agreed that a working notion of what is meant by culture is essential to their conceptual and descriptive work. Yet they have not achieved consensus about the meaning of "culture." Instead, culture theory continues to be an arena of feisty contention in anthropology.

During the past two decades the dominant concepts of culture have borrowed their shapes from linguistic theory. These concepts include the structuralist accounts articulated by Levi-Strauss and his followers, as well as similar theories developed by American semanticists. Structuralism provides abstract models of imputed regulative structures and mechanisms whose orderly workings generate concrete patterns. The key distinction in structuralism is between the "deep" level, or the regulative principles, and the "surface" level, or concrete arenas of thought and activity which these principles generate from the raw materials of the world. This way of thinking not only resembles the structuralist linguistics of Jakobson and others, but also modern molecular biology (where nucleic acid structures, when biochemically activated, are seen as generating concrete life forms; encoded in such structures are information systems with teleonomic trajectories[1]). As successful as structuralist linguistics and molecular biology have been, I believe that applying such thinking to the study of human culture has been a wasted and misguided effort. No one has convincingly demonstrated that domains of human ideas and activities are structured in the manner of language, or, for that matter, that they are really "structured" at all. Chomsky, whose efforts to develop models of grammar have often been cited by anthropologists as a source of their own theories, has clearly repudiated the integrity of a structuralist concept of culture, arguing that language is a *distinctively* designed system whose forms are biological in origin, and whose creative aspect is somatic. Efforts to view culture as being like language are off the mark (Chomsky 1968, 1975).

While one problem with the discourse about the concept of culture has been excessive abstraction and model building, the other has been reification. Put simply, it is *activity* which is concrete (including the activity called "thinking," as Geertz has so convincingly argued), not culture. A key problem with the use of the concept of culture has been the attempt to link cultures with social units or groupings, thereby reifying cultural boundaries between such groupings. It is easy to understand this temptation and error, since whenever we talk about anything cultural we seek to demarcate it and contrast its features with something else. What often happens in this attempt is that such boundaries are made to seem overly firm. We arrive at the sorts of cultural units which are suitable for inventory or mapping, but which often seem detached from the social reality from which they are derived and fail to reflect that particular reality's actual dimensions. This is the perennial difficulty of positivism and perhaps it is unavoidable. We often need to break up reality into "things" so we can comprehend it, but often we select the wrong things or misunderstand them.

Another way to understand social reality is to look for pattern in style. Style may be read in the ambience of social events and settings. This is what we do when we wish to get a sense of the "tone" and contours of a scene. Here the skills the ethnographer needs to bring to the field are more like those of the attuned journalist, the filmmaker, or the documentary photographer than of the natural scientist confidently seeking to discover a discrete order in what he knows is a rule-bound universe.

When we look at a cultural setting or a social event we are struck by an intricately textured morass suitably conceived of by Geertz as requiring "thick description." We always risk misinterpretation. But we cannot avoid this by falling back on some more "formal" mode of analysis promising unambiguous precision as its outcome. The world is ambiguous and as ethnographers we must face that fact and make the most of it. The people whose activities we follow are shifting and inconsistent, and through their actions they reveal the many facets of their intentions. Therefore, it is best to carefully follow and note the action which engages the social participants whose movements we wish to clarify. Positivism in its greed for "facts" demands data which, ideally, is quantifiable. Interpreting social style precludes exactness as a criterion for successful analysis. We can only hope to illuminate and evoke. But such an outlook, no less than positivism, can yield explanation or, perhaps more precisely, explication. It is possible to unravel social threads much as a critic seeks to unravel the meanings of a text.

To accomplish this, we should not approach sociocultural patterns as though they were discrete structures. The structuralist method of approaching a cultural "text" as though its structure could be revealed by subjecting the text to a sequence of discrete analytical operations has had very limited success, particularly in regard to understanding social action. We need to explore the ambiguous shape of society by illumination rather than analysis. We want to shed light on a variety of social forms rather than discover their elusive essence.

This book will look at the social circumstances and outlooks of Afro-Trinidadian urban men. I hope to illuminate how such men have examined their social pasts and assessed their present conditions and how, from their assessments, they have come to articulate their intentions and judgments.

If we adopt a style of research where the key event is the encounter between the ethnographer as an investigator and people as actors, then the pivotal question becomes: how do we select and assemble our interpretive frames? Goffman, borrowing and elaborating Bateson's ideas on the framing of communicative events, has argued that the manner in which the ethnographer assembles his impressions of events involves identifying the events according to the principles of organization that govern them, *together with* our subjective involvement in those events (Goffman 1974:26). One key dimension of such involvement includes our ability to "read" a performance, to see it as genuine or straight expression, as drama or play, as duplicity or sincerity. Long ago Goffman pointed out the important difference between the impression a person *gives,* and that one which he *gives off* (1959:2); that is the difference between the intentional conveyance of information to a listener, and the listener's ability to look beyond intent and notice various cues in behavioral display, some of which may contradict intentionally conveyed information and appearances. One program with an approach that involves the formal interviewing of informants on a scheduled basis (and this has been a key mode of ethnographic investigation), is that the ethnographer acquires supposedly genuine information with little opportunity to assess its validity.

As I conducted fieldwork in Trinidad, informants, even those with whom I had developed a rapport, often made statements or gave answers that were discredited by statements I overheard them make to others soon after. As "informants" the people we encounter during fieldwork often try to polish things up for us; and we cannot really blame them, as we recognize how peculiar it is for a stranger to ask intimate questions and expect truthful answers. In ethnographic work, one has to become attuned to the impressions people intentionally convey, some of which are pressed upon the ethnographer with a compelling urgency and are often suspect for that very reason, as well as those which they unintentionally give off and some- times attempt to conceal. Some assessment of ethnographic truth emerges from examining all layers of statement and behavioral display, from those that are openly revealed to those that are carefully concealed. Out of such assembled impressions much of what makes up an ethnography develops its shape. In the following chapters I describe people and scenes in what has often been viewed disparagingly as an "impressionistic" manner. Certainly in view of positivistic standards of verifiability such a manner is unaccept- able. But even the most formal and rigorous of ethnographers cannot escape the fact that much of their descriptive and explanatory work amounts to something like "from what I saw and heard it seemed to me that things were like this and like that." The debate here is not whether one should adopt a scientific or a humanistic approach; these are not incompatible and, in fact, ultimately become harmonious. But if we are going to be scientific about social activity and experience that we cannot be as scientific about it as we are about language or biology. The observational and descriptive focus of natural history has gone out of fashion as other modes of biological reasoning and fact collection have come into prominence; but to comprehend human activity—and its absolutely key elements of consciousness and intention—we can never go beyond a naturalistic approach; we can only supplement it.

This book is primarily about urban lifestyles in Trinidad, not about culture theory. The preceding pages have been an opportunity to establish a point of view regarding the assumptions that propel me to practice ethnog- raphy. Every description of society, however casual—from a travel writer's report on what to look for in Rio's Carnival, to the most abstruse accounts of multisectional kinship systems—contains an implicit outlook on culture and social experience. I conducted the fieldwork upon which this book is based in Port-of-Spain, Trinidad in 1969, and again in 1970–1971 (fifteen months altogether). I visited briefly in the winter of 1978–1979. Things have changed somewhat and here and there I note my impressions of such changes. Afro-Caribbean culture is four centuries old; I wish here to provide a glimpse of that culture as I experienced it a few years ago. Funds supporting my research were provided by the Yale University Council on Latin American Studies and the National Science Foundation.

Thanks are due to a number of people for their help and guidance, fore- most to Sidney Mintz, my teacher at Yale. Mintz exemplifies what I mean by the importance of wisdom and insight above any neatly packaged theoretical or methodological outlook. To me he has always seemed to be right on the mark in his thinking and work. Also, much appreciation goes to Anthony Maingot, a Trinidadian and another teacher at Yale, whose personal vibrancy gave me an early hint of the energy of Trinidadian society. My thanks also to Ira Lowenthal, a friend and colleague who has been consistently a source of inspiration; and to Kai Erikson, who read this book when it was still a doctoral dissertation and encouraged its publication. Three great scholars—Gregory Bateson, Clifford Geertz and Erving Goffman—have, by their spectacular insights, contributed to opening the windows of my mind, and I offer them enduring thanks and appreciation. Finally, for all those Trinidadians who shared their lives and insights, and good and bad times with me, an embrace.

Chapter 1

The Background

Three factors, combined into a sociohistorical amalgam, account for the distinctiveness of the Caribbean ambience.

First, as a sociocultural region the Caribbean developed in what may be called a vacuum of indigenousness. The earliest European settlers, through outright extermination and the introduction of Old World diseases, were remarkably successful in depopulating the area of its aboriginal inhabitants, leaving, here and there, marginal groups of Indians whose impact on the cultural future would be virtually nonexistent. This became no Great Plains or Andean region where European and North American conquerers gradually encircled, controlled, used and abused, and finally discarded as cultural refuse the aboriginal populations. In most of North and South America the whites used the aborigines as labor in various exploitive enterprises, or drove them into sharply delimited niches where their movements would not interfere with free expansion and where their actions could be monitored by hostile administrators. In the Caribbean, however, where Indian populations were wiped out with remarkable thoroughness in one of the less heralded episodes of human genocide, imperialistic intrusion and expansion throughout the region could proceed as though the area were simply a cluster of *lands,* without a human or cultural presence. From the conquest on, the history of the Caribbean has been the history of imported peoples.

Secondly, the Caribbean was first and foremost a region of overseas agricapitalist development, one of the early experiments of European colonialism and a generally successful one. In the Caribbean, Europeans learned the important lesson that homeland interests could be made to prosper by a thorough and efficient exploitation of overseas colonies and their resources. While initial Spanish hegemony was based largely on the exploitation of gold and silver resources, later British, French and Dutch hegemonies were grounded in the success of Caribbean sugar production. And the profitability of sugar was itself based on a unique system of exploitation: the slave-based plantation. The New World plantation, from its very beginnings, was a very "modern" institution, its design streamlined for efficient production and high profitability. These two aims were achieved through the use of imported African slave labor. The plantation system as a mode of production, together with slave labor as the force of production, set the stage for the development of Caribbean society. Most key features of Afro-Caribbean cultural patterns must be understood against the background of the plantation and its organizational contingencies. The legacy of the plantation system includes majority populations of African descent, economic brittleness and rigidity as a consequence of the plantation system's strangulation of viable economic alternatives, and a deep-rooted cynicism concerning the supposed wonders of Euro-Caucasian life and culture together with the inescapable effects of such cultural influences on Caribbean developments.

Thirdly, the Caribbean has developed as an arena of ethnic diversity. The first stage in the composition of this ethnic mosaic involved the coming together of several different European populations with African slaves of various tribal origins. The second stage, following the abolition of slavery, involved the introduction of assorted ethnic groups—Indians, Chinese, Middle Eastern peoples, Indochinese, Javanese—as replacements for the labor lost, and the consequent formation of ethnic enclaves. Another key factor in the construction of this mosaic was the formation of new groups or social categories through ethnic blending, the most important of these being mulatto or "colored" groups formed through successive European and African admixtures. Demographically then, Caribbean societies present poly-ethnic patterns of residence and sociality. Concern with ethnicity has continued to reverberate through Caribbean ideology and politics, and such concern has woven its way into social relations in innumerable ways.

An Abbreviated Sociology of the Caribbean

Several features have come to characterize the Caribbean region as a result of these peculiar historical developments.

Since the economies, and the accompanying politics, of the Caribbean have, from their inception, been highly capitalistic in organization, class-based stratification has arisen to an elaborate degree. Moreover, a poly-ethnic spectrum has become a feature of most of the Caribbean, and this has meant that race and ethnic relations have taken on a particular importance in social life. With the extension and elaboration of class- and ethnic-based differences, sociocultural styles have developed in competition with each other, and certain styles have taken on a "mainstream" status, while others have been condemned and belittled. In the past those styles associated with a European-focused elite have constituted the mainstream, while those associated with the Afro-Caribbean mass of the population have been denigrated and forced to respond to the intrusions of that mainstream. This state of affairs has come under sharp attack in recent times.

Those groups who in the past ruled, and today continue to dominate the islands—namely Caucasians, Europeans, and "colored"—retained a great deal of control over what sorts of social arrangements, ideologies, commitments and behavioral styles were acceptable, and which were not. That is, they defined a legitimate cultural domain (what I will call a *mainstream*) and repudiated other domains. Most significantly, they attempted, and to some extent succeeded, to back up their cultural preferences with political clout. This conforms to the usual colonialist pattern, where the legitimization and enforcement of cultural preferences typically become woven into political intentions because those who administer and govern are usually very different, ethnically and socially, from those who are subjected to their administrative control.

Within such an ambience problems of national identity formation have been accordingly severe. With no precolonial indigenous traditions available as partial models for the construction of a postcolonial society (as has been possible in much of the rest of the Third World), the attempt to forge an image of such a society is limited to reconstructions and elaborations of the repertory set down by the colonial experience. Occasionally some group attempts to transcend such limitations, as in the case of the Rastafarians of Jamaica who have chosen to reject the entire colonial experience and its modern residues as one immense malignancy, focusing instead on what they claim to be a pure distillation of Africanness without Euro-American pollutions.[2] Their attempt to create a cultural alternative has been gallant and spectacular, and in many ways successful, but a combination of mythical attachments and apocalyptic visions cannot be the materials out of which to forge a modern national identity. This is not to condemn such attachments or visions; it just may be that a modern nation state, freed from the polluting and corroding effects of the colonialist experience, is not an easy possibility to realize; a genuine integrity of purpose and lifestyle may remain unachievable within the constraints of the nation state.

In the Caribbean such gloomy prospects are heightened by the poor economic and political condition of most of the islands. The islands can barely sustain themselves economically, and yet it has been impossible for them to combine in one way or another to create new polities or inter-island economic arrangements. Hence dependency has continued to be a major motif of the Caribbean ambience. The islands are dependent on metropolitan powers who continue to maintain one or another mode of control—a willingness to continue sending down tourists, for example. Or one island may depend on other islands, creating an asymmetrical condition which leaves the smaller islands pawns in political manipulations over which they have very little control. All of this, in one way or another, reflects the utter dependence of the Caribbean on the control structures of overseas corporations and other external economic contingencies.

Alienation virtually oozes out of all the fissures of Caribbean social structure. Power-holding groups tend to be deeply alienated from anything resembling a grass roots national consciousness—usually of proletarian origin—but maintain firm political control. The masses are alienated from bourgeois lifestyles which are imposed on them in various overt and covert ways, as appropriate designs for living. In one sense few regions on earth have been more affected by North American styles, demands, needs and other metropolitan images of the way life should be lived. But the resources necessary for living this sort of life are not available to the bulk of the Caribbean population, a classic case of the wide gap between aspirations and possibilities which has been such a key legacy of the colonial experience. But, in another sense, Caribbean peoples have maintained a remarkable resiliency of adaptive response and a tenacity of commitment to purely internal demands in spite of an overbearing colonialist presence. It is this aspect in particular that I want to emphasize in this book. While so much of the world has succumbed to the Western ideal of material success, many black West Indians have held on to their alternatives and their answers, these at least partly stemming from a continuing hold and appeal of African priorities. For the Rastafarians provide only an extreme version of a deeply held Caribbean sentiment: that perhaps the Western pie in the sky and its earthly demands are no blessing at all, for where is the soul and the compassion of such a culture?[2]

More than one observer has noted the individualistic character of Caribbean social life. Particularly coming from anthropologists, such observations need to be appropriately framed. The ethnographic experience has for the most part been with peoples who have been overwhelmingly communitarian in the arrangement of social activities, such activities usually being the work of formal groupings of one sort or another—lineages, age grades, residential units. In the Caribbean, the group-based organization of activity has been no less a feature of the social landscape; but group formation has taken on a less formal and more ad hoc character. Slavery and subsequent socioeconomic developments have not destroyed community life and instead created an individualistic atomism, as ethnographers sometimes have claimed. Rather, communal life, at least among black populations, has developed more fluid forms.

Caribbean social conditions have created an ambience where the individual's adaptive flexibility in seeking out suitable and advantageous arrangements and linkages is at a premium. This sometimes creates the impression that communal orientations have only weakly developed. A more accurate assessment would look toward the special contingencies that have compelled distinctive patterns of social organization based on the advantages of such flexibilty to emerge. Rather than looking for crisply delineated groupings and structures, it is more useful to seek out the sources of social rapport that have brought people together into such loosely woven, easy—to—rearrange cooperative units as the much maligned and misnamed "matrifocal family." Viewed in this way, individualism and ad hoc group formation are linked as motifs reflecting Caribbean social conditions. Much of this book will seek to explore some dimensions of such links.

An Abbreviated Social History of Trinidad

Trinidad emerged as a full-blown colony producing sugar for export to Europe later than most of the islands. Further, such development occurred in a context where there was a transfer of power from one European nation to another *after* certain social forms had already become consolidated. The Spanish were the first to occupy Trinidad, but their interest in this island and their other Caribbean possessions began to wane as the allure of South American mineral resources became vastly more attractive. But the Spanish, aware that any future development of the island depended on the availability of a viable population, opened Trinidad up for immigration, offering generous land grants to settlers. Planters with their slaves came from Haiti and the other French islands in large numbers, bringing with them their highly developed technical knowledge of sugar cultivation. Once sugar became firmly established in Trinidad, the import of slaves began on a large scale. During this period, when Trinidad was joining the other islands in supporting a slave-based plantation society, the French influence was paramount. The British captured Trinidad during the Napoleonic wars, and Spain ceded the territory to Britain in 1802. The island remained in British hands until independence in 1962, when it became a member of the British Commonwealth (it has recently become a republic). By the time the British gained control, a Creole way of life, largely based on Spanish and French influences, had taken hold in Trinidad, and in many respects Britain had only limited impact on the island's cultural development in its century and a half of possession. Even before the abolition of slavery and the introduction of several other ethnic populations into the island as contracted labor, Trinidad was already a multiplex society; interwoven through its mosaic was the diverse impact of an African, a Spanish, a French and a British presence. Spanish legal codes continued to maintain a hold even after the British takeover. Spanish and French remained established languages for some while, and even today some Trinidadians continue to speak both Spanish and a French-based Creole language. There were similar effects on the development of a cuisine, which is consequently one of the more interesting in the

Caribbean. Spanish and French styles have had their impact on architecture and city planning, and they have enriched the extremely broad musical repertoire of the island. And to all this must be added the most paramount influence of all: African slaves and their immensely rich cultural styles. Out of all this a unique Creole cultural stew slowly simmered, and Trinidad consequently lacks the single, rather distinct colonial flavor of such societies as Barbados, Haiti and Cuba.

Slavery was abolished by the British in England in 1834 and its abolishment affected in Trinidad in 1838. The British then discouraged free blacks from engaging in agriculture and becoming peasant farmers, wishing to insure their continued availability as laborers. The free slaves shunned the prospect of remaining on the sugar plantations though, partly because the slave experience had attached a strong social stigma to agricultural labor. The sugar plantocracy then had the British government subsidize the immigration of laborers to Trinidad under a contract system. Initial attempts were made to use Chinese and Portuguese laborers, but these attempts were largely unsuccessful as those groups quickly turned to commerce and away from agricultural work. But beginning in 1845, and continuing for over seventy years, the British brought about 145,000 Indians to Trinidad from various parts of the Indian subcontinent. Since the mid-nineteenth century, then, Indians replaced African slaves in the sugar fields, becoming Trinidad's plantation proletariat in the process. Somewhat later, numbers of Middle Eastern immigrants, primarily from Syria and Lebanon, began to enter the island in significant numbers, and these groups turned to commercial activity almost immediately.

Colonial and ethnic succession have meant that a number of different cultural traditions were introduced into the island, accounting for the striking ethnic and stylistic diversity that is such a paramount feature of the Trinidadian social landscape. Today the descendents of African slaves and Indian immigrants account for over ninety percent of the population, Indians slightly outnumbering blacks. The remainder of the population includes the descendents of Chinese and Middle Eastern immigrants, as well as those of European descent.

The plantation system never took as firm a hold in Trinidad as it did in many of the other islands. This had to do in part with the nature of effective colonization of the island, occurring as it did a good deal later than elsewhere in the Caribbean, and after the pivotal importance of the sugar economy had already peaked. Trinidad's rugged terrain and rain forest cover also imposed difficulties on attempts to establish an effective system of plantations. Furthermore, the scant population of the island during the eighteenth century created a chronic labor shortage. More recently, Trinidad, alone in the Caribbean, was found to contain exploitable petroleum resources, and with the exploitation of these resources and their central importance in the Trinidadian economy, the country has become much less an agrarian society. Altogether then, Trinidad, unlike most of the Caribbean region, has never been overwhelmingly agrarian. And a turn away from agrarianism has had important consequences on the development of the island's social forms, affecting the rapid development of a proletarian segment; the emergence of urbanism; the rise of political consciousness and cosmopolitanism; skepticism in attitudes toward work and economic "improvement;" inventiveness in the fluid arrangements of residential styles, and so forth. Today sugar cultivation is becoming more and more peripheral, as is the cultivation of other crops. Oil production and refining are the backbone of the Trinidadian economy, involving a larger segment of the labor force than any other mode of production and generating enormous revenues.

One consequence of the focus on industry and the growth of the proletariat has been the emergence of forceful, militant, often clearly Marxist labor unions and with this the development of finely articulated political ideologies. Militant trade unionism exploded in the oil fields of south and central Trinidad during the 1930s. At a time when other British territories were more quiescent than rebellious, Trinidad shook with violent turmoil as strikes and states of emergency sent the colony into a paroxysm of political crisis. Trinidadian radicalism spread to the other islands and, even in recent years, since independence, political leaders throughout the Caribbean have viewed Trinidad as a hotbed of radicalism, promising to politically contaminate what they often, and usually erroneously, suppose to be their rather more stable societies.

During the disturbances of the 1930s, a political consciousness associated with racial hostility began to emerge in the industrial sector. The urban proletariat was much more aware than were rural workers of the economic gaps which divided the mass of the population from the superordinate, dominant elites. That is, Trinidadian radicalism tended to be an urban, industrial phenomenon, while the tensions emerging from the rapidly changing industrial ambience of the 1930s remained more muted in rural districts where, apart from poorer and more ragged networks of political communication, relationships based on kinship and religious ties ran deeper and stronger, interfering with a class-based ideological consolidation. Furthermore, the urban-industrial crystallization of political recognitions and tensions was propelled by the magnification of interclass and interethnic hostilities within a social terrain carved up out of juxtaposed and highly differentiated residential areas. That is, in the towns and cities people who often distrusted and despised each other found themselves living in close proximity, constantly scrutinizing each others' moves with suspicious and accusing eyes. This has continued to be a key characteristic of the urban ambience of Trinidad. In short, what was happening during the 1930s was the growing predominance of urban life and, with it, an attendent growth of ethnic and class hostilities, as well as the concommitant radicalization of Black industrial workers.

Ethnic hostilities, though rooted partially in the initial contacts between ethnic groups in the nineteenth century, grew in magnitude and intensity with the proletarianization of Trinidad's black population. While a black, industrial sector increasingly pursued socialist goals, a rural East Indian agrarian proletariat and peasantry repudiated those goals and differentiated itself from the black industrial population. In short, as class realities began to appear more salient to Afro-Americans, so ethnic realities reasserted themselves as key determinants of East Indian ideological stances. To the East Indians, the politicization of a large portion of the black population only meant that an ethnic segment, already distrusted, was mobilizing its political resources, thereby promising to become even more worrisome a prospect in the arena of ethnic competition. Furthermore, strong East Indian commitments to family, village and religion precluded the appeal of a socialist-radical interpretation of events and, for many, such an interpretation was made to seem even more threatening by various chauvinist fearmongers. These "voices" of the East Indian community often worked in close association with members of the white elite who were only too eager to stir up a fear of socialism and of blacks among East Indians, thereby further polarizing ethnic differences and hoping to defuse the nightmare prospect of an East Indian and black coalition pivoted around socialist and anticolonialist goals. Ethnic polarization has continued as a major political theme in Trinidad, and was vividly reenacted in the political disturbances of the early 1970s when the East Indian population remained aloof and detached from the political fervor that embroiled other sectors.

During the 1930s a modern and highly articulated political consciousness emerged in Trinidad. In the 1940s modernization arose from a very different source. Since World War II one of the dominant features of Trinidadian national style has been the impact of North American influence. This influence arose out of the American military presence on the island during the War, and it has had an enormous impact on the physical face and on the socioeconomic contours of the island. While the Americans occupied the naval base at Chaguaramas their physical presence was overwhelming, particularly over the heavily populated northwestern sector of the island. The base and other American facilities served as major employers and deeply affected employment on the island. American wages were usually much higher than those available from local business concerns, but those concerns also prospered through their many dealings with the base. American servicemen had large amounts of cash to spend and they spent it, as they usually do, on their pleasures. This encouraged the proliferation of small commerce of all sorts, particularly of bars and nightclubs and brothels. With the American presence, wheeler-dealers of various sorts prospered magnificently and some of the great Trinidadian fortunes were made at this time. The Americans left the island after Eric Williams, the first Prime Minister of a postindependence government, carried out his promise to evict them from Chaguaramas, and a large and reliable source of income suddenly vanished for many Trinidadians.

Not only were American military personnel excellent sources of exploitable income, but their presence left its cultural imprints. Trinidadians began to emulate things American, particularly in contrast to newly-ridiculed, though long-resented British styles and motifs. Movies, tremendously popular in Trinidad since the introduction of the first commercial cinema, continually presented various glamorous images of American ways to Trinidadians. The arrival of so many Americans during the war served further to affect an Americanization of many aspects of the Trinidadian national scene.

A more recent source of North American influence has been the steady Americanization of the Trinidadian economy. The oil industry quickly came to be dominated by American and international corporations such as Shell and Texaco. American managers, engineers and technical personnel have been all over the island and they have left their mark. The establishment of local branches of American and Canadian businesses has been, in recent years, the single most important feature of industrial and commercial growth on the island. With the proliferation of such firms and their often American-dominated managing staffs, the Trinidadian economy has more and more become a by-product of North American overseas industrial investment, as in the past it was a by-product of European economic plans and interventions. All of this has had its effects, many of which are as ugly as one would expect to emerge from such developments, and threaten to erode Trinidadian independence and distinctiveness further. What all of this has meant to the average Trinidadian is that he is likely to be buying American brand-name consumer goods; he is bombarded with American advertising using American models and portraying such typically American scenes as the blonde with the can of 7-Up on the carefully manicured lawn of her ranch-style home. These images serve as vehicles for ideas of desirable, but—for most Trinidadians—unachievable, lifestyles. A worker's bosses, at one level or another, may very well be Americans or Canadians. Altogether, Trinidadians have come to associate business and consumption patterns with an American way of life which they have then tried to emulate, or find themselves trapped within, or—as has happened more and more in recent years—sharply criticize and repudiate.

Trinidadians view television shows, see movies and read magazines that originate in the United States; local media play second fiddle to the imported American product. A Port-of-Spain resident may know more about what is happening in Brooklyn than he knows about what is happening in southern

Trinidad. But those in the south of Trinidad are likely to be in touch with Port-of-Spain developments, partly because they know that it is in the capital city where American styles make their Trinidadian debut.

This is only half the picture. Not only does the American mainstream have its effects on the development of a Trinidadian mainstream, but "counter-mainstream" American styles are often adopted and fused with counter-mainstream Trinidadian styles. This is true of ideological and political perspectives, fashion, music and so forth. In such developments there is much more promise. They involve the possibility of a sort of international rapport among segments of national populations that are able to articulate the insufficiences or contradictions of mainstream notions in their own societies and learn from the ways other societies have repudiated these notions and developed alternatives to them. Much of this, of course, has happened as a consequence of West Indian migrations to North America and subsequent returns to the island. The Jamaican, Marcus Garvey, best epitomizes such effects; his influence and presence have spanned and fused a Caribbean consciousness with a North American one.

In Trinidad, convincing national art forms, which perhaps more than anything have been responsible for the emergence of a distinctly Trinidadian esthetic ambience, have developed. Though emulation and even mimicry of American and European art forms is widespread and continues to influence local cultural concerns strongly (especially among bourgeois "artistes" and their admirers), indigenous music, dance, folklore and, more recently, theater impart an especially lively and jovial quality to the artistic life of the island. Perhaps it is during Carnival, the quintessential Trinidadian event, that the power and style of Trinidadian life is most clearly and evocatively displayed. Here calypso, the steelband, folk theater and varieties of dance and display blend in the production of an event which pulses with a distinctively Trinidadian beat and shines with a distinctively Trinidadian radiance.

Recent Developments

During the past decade Trinidad has been faced with a series of national crises that have called into question the effectiveness of the government's efforts to stimulate a healthy development of the society and to alleviate persistent problems. From many points of view, the People's National Movement, the dominant political party since independence, and its leader and guiding spirit, Dr. Eric Williams, failed to come to grips with what has seemed to many to be an increasing tendency for the country to stagnate socio-economically, and to fail to extricate itself from foreign economic and political domination. With the growth of an antigovernment grass roots political consciousness during the 1960s, the Trinidadian establishment found itself more severely condemned and distrusted than ever before. Strikes and other expressions of discontent increased in frequency and in fervor, and states of emergency were subsequently imposed, disrupting the rather artificial political and economic quietude the government had hoped to maintain. In 1970 political tensions exploded in a series of events which saw the status quo shattered as the government and business elites confronted a leftist black nationalist coalition which was far more militant in its demands than previous radical movements. This coalition of discontent, which became known collectively as the Black Power Movement, was a rather unlikely amalgam of groups and organizations which, in one way or another, found the situation in Trinidad to be increasingly intolerable. This amalgam included, and continues to include, university radicals and academic Marxists, leftist labor unions, dissident factions within the armed forces, black nationalist groups, and a rather amorphous lumpen-proletarian and street-based conglomeration of neighborhood, youth and ethnic groups.

The riots and demonstrations that exploded during the first quarter of 1970, and government-imposed curfew and state of emergency afterward, had their roots in a number of events, including several very tense labor crises, power struggles within the military ranks, and the Canadian government's persecution of Trinidadian students as a result of racially-tinged incidents at Sir George Williams University in Montreal. Racial and ethnic conflict were central themes in these disturbances but other kinds of conflict —over employment, civil liberties, economic stagnation—were expressed in racial and ethnic terms. Underlying the direct causes of the 1970 outbreak and the seemingly racial character of that outbreak was the apparent failure of the government's social and economic policies, and a public recognition that these policies did not add up to what the government intended or portrayed them to be. The critics pointed out two outstanding features as characteristic of the Trinidadian condition: the high and growing rate of unemployment, particularly among youths, and the continuing and deepening external domination of the economy by international corporations allied with residues of the old colonial economic elite. The analysis was rather simple and to the point: when the going was good, foreign-controlled industrial and agricultural concerns provided large numbers of jobs, albeit under paternalistic conditions, but when the going got rough, it became all too clear that these same concerns had very little interest in what was beneficial to Trinidad and its working people. Their commitment to the island's economy depended solely on the expectation of continuing profits. When such commitment was no longer possible—and during the 1960s it became clear that it was becoming less and less possible, particularly in the case of sugar—these enterprises responded by laying off workers in large numbers. This all too clearly reminded critics of the schemes and shifts of the old sugar plantocracy. It, too, had no commitment to the society as a whole. When the profitability of sugar production diminished, interests were turned elsewhere, striking the first critical blow against Trinidadian social viability.

The critics also felt that the government's attempts to industrialize the island further by encouraging monopoly capitalism through development schemes that held out truly extravagant rewards to potential investors were no more than a continuing program to retain control of the economy by white local capitalists in the interests of white foreign investors. For all of the talk of absorbing the island's growing labor force through the encouragement of industry, it became quite clear to many that no such consequences were visible. To the contrary, the government's programs of promised economic improvement resulted in a further deterioration of national economic viability, as such viability was reflected in a satisfied labor force. And, the critics contended, while the government was serving foreign business interests, it was simultaneously introducing such antilabor legislation as measures to outlaw strikes, and generally tried to tame labor as much as possible.

I will not outline here the actual steps leading to the outbreak of disturbances, but during the early part of 1970 extensive demonstrations, marches, and occasional riots broke out through Trinidad, particularly in Port-of-Spain. Though the protest was serious, it could hardly be said to have created a revolutionary situation. But the government and the bourgeoisie panicked, and the turmoil which did arise within the military was interpreted as an attempt to overthrow the government. The United States and Venezuelan navies flexed their muscles, indicating their "concern" over potentially revolutionary developments and threatening (with the memory of Cuba always in mind), through a show of force, that no such development would be allowed to gain much momentum. The government responded with repressive measures and extensive arrests. The tensions eventually subsided, but Trinidad emerged from all of this a political shambles. In 1970 Eric Williams and the PNM again won an election, but this election was, for practical purposes, uncontested, and the level of confidence the public had in the government and in their once-Messiah, Dr. Williams, was badly eroded.

Meanwhile, the problems continue today: unemployment; a continuing alienation of the black (and especially young) proletariat from the middle classes and their North American outlooks; complex racial tensions involving the black and white sector, and blacks and East Indians; failure to stabilize the economy or increase its productivity; and conflict between lifestyles as those who are black and poor begin to realize more and more that there is no reason for them to emulate the aspirations of a hostile bourgeoisie. Whether the seemingly new bonus of vastly increased revenues from petroleum resources will significantly alter this situation remains to be seen.

In the Caribbean, those who are the descendents of African slaves and view themselves and are viewed by others as being black, have always been in the majority. But this Afro-Caribbean sector has been kept, first through slavery and then through less dramatic though equally effective modes of oppression, subordinate to the European population and its Creole descendents. The institutions, values, rules and ideas of the white sector have been imposed as morally proper and innately superior, and have come to constitute what I have referred to as a mainstream. Such imposition has been backed by political and legal force. But the values laid down by the white sector are not the only ones operable or available as standards for the design of Caribbean commitments. They have been joined by the very different values and priorities of the subordinate population. As a consequence, a duality has come to characterize Caribbean social life. On the one hand, there are the premises of the European-established institutional order and its attendant values. On the other hand, there exists a multiplicity of special sociocultural values and norms reflecting particular adaptations made by politically subordinate West Indians to the persistence of a politically and economically difficult environment and its contradictions and pressures. Some of these ideas and notions arose specifically in contrast to the superimposed structure. Others are residual, though persistent and often effective carryovers from pre-Caribbean traditions. The Caribbean social order takes its shape from such multiple influences and developments. In the following chapters I wish to explore some dimensions of this set of conditions as they may be revealed through an examination of concrete lives, events and activities.

Chapter 2

The Setting

A visitor to a new setting, whether an ethnographer or a more casual traveler, often tends to view that setting and its people and activities as more homogeneous than it eventually turns out to be. A visitor at first telescopes a variety of features which, taken together, seem to strike him as different from his familiar terrain. He tends to see a vague and undifferentiated new forest rather than new varieties of trees. But as he becomes more sensitive to a new setting and more familiar with its contours, he begins to draw distinctions and make contrasts among themes and elements which seemed lost in the amorphousness of first impressions. Analysis is a process whereby the initial gestalt ("this is a slum," "these are black people," "this is poverty") is rearranged and reorganized so that its contrasting features and details become more apparent. Emerging from such a process may be the recognition that the initial gestalt was invalid. Or it may continue to seem generally valid but require further elaboration, refinement or articulation. A successful outcome still leaves one with a unified gestalt, rather than the debris of analytical breakdown, but the gestalt seems more compelling and more comprehensive.

Urban ethnography amounts to something rather different from the ethnography conducted by anthropologists in the relatively insulated and undifferentiated communities that have been their characteristic domains of field study. Consequently, the ethnographic approach to the study of city life must depart at least somewhat from many of the usual assumptions. A typical ethnography involves the study of a small number of interconnected people in a delineated residential setting. But in a city the numbers are large; the connections are fluid and diffused; and the residential setting often seems more like a maze than a community.

The community study bias, so prevalent in anthropology, creates problems when carried over to the study of urban life. I carried this bias with me to Trinidad, as I initially looked for ways in which I could carve up the scene so as to locate and isolate for myself a locus or zone for research—a "typical" proletarian neighborhood, for example. But increasingly this did not seem to be the best solution, considering the sort of place Port-of-Spain turned out to be and my interests in finding out certain things about the city. I was too focused on finding a *place* within which I could conduct my research, and lost sight of the fact that finding and sticking to such a place would undermine other more important concerns: discovering what directions the *flow* of social life takes in an urban context.

While I realized that neighborhoods could often be viewed as sub-community units to be described in terms of their formal social organization (ethnography provides many examples of such arrangements), this was certainly not nearly so true of Port-of-Spain. My interest was in assessing how poor black men spent their time and organized their activities and I began to recognize that for many young Port-of-Spain men, the spatial coincidence of work, residence, family life, friendships, amusements, and political and religious involvement was limited. A man lived here, worked there and entertained himself somewhere else. He floated in one direction to see his family, other directions to hang out with his friends. He *moved*, he spread himself outward. If following the flow of action meant following such outward movements, then to focus on a single ethnographic space (the "locale" of fieldwork) would do little justice to the social reality at hand, hindering and restricting a flexibility which I felt was necessary and appropriate.

I realized I could not conveniently carve out an ethnographic space and set out to learn as much as I could about what went on within that space. Such a convenience belied a reality, and that reality required a different mode of operation. It is in making the ethnographic choices (What space will my observations and work encompass?) that the problem of reification first emerges. I recognized I need not be so concerned with boundaries. Where a people's activities and commitments are dispersed, often in a helter-skelter manner, then the ethnographer's fieldwork, observations and reportage must likewise be dispersed. Nevertheless, I describe neighborhoods in this chapter, not so much because they are suitable units for investigation, but because they are aspects of the overall social scenario. Neighborhoods are settings within which social activities take place; they are not "natural" units of sociological study which demarcate the limits of activities to be investigated. Anthropologists have usually first selected settings and then gone on to describe patterns of social activity within those settings. Sometimes this seems a suitable rationale; sometimes it is not. For me, and for an accurate description of Trinidadian society, it was not. The problem with selecting a setting is that the choice of a setting predetermines the range of activities to which the ethnographer exposes himself. Instead, one may place initial emphasis on activities, rather than on locales, and doing this seemed much more appropriate to me. I felt it was a matter of "feeling around" rather than "pinning myself down."

Port-of-Spain

To a North American, accustomed to his own urban ambience—in New York, in Toronto, in Chicago or in San Francisco—Port-of-Spain seems like a very different sort of place. It is shabbier, louder, livelier, more intimate; its action and pace seem more fluid, less jagged. Most of all, it is full of animation and sound: people talking, making music and listening to it, dancing, arguing and joking. And nearly all of this happens outdoors, not within private confines, but out in the public arena of the streets, alleyways and yards.

Port-of-Spain is the capital of a country which is becoming increasingly more urban in character. It contains about 150,000 people, most of whom are of African ancestry. It is a poor city, but it is also where most of Trinidad's bourgeoisie lives. Its tone is distinctively Caribbean and distinctively Trinidadian, but here and there, and increasingly, it seems, there are touches of North American influence: discotheques, fried chicken joints reminiscent of Colonel Sander's shops, discount houses of every imaginable sort, "lounges"; in short, those North American contributions for which social science does not seem to have a suitable idiom but which are well summed up by everyday idiom as being "plastic" and "tacky."

The city faces south toward the Gulf of Paria which separates Trinidad from Venezuela, and runs more east and west than north and south, a consequence of its expansion along the waterfront. Much of the city is flat, but as it extends northward, eastward and northwestward it becomes hillier, and along its northern edge the city is surrounded by fairly steep and heavily forested hills. Suburbs ring the city and beyond these suburbs lies a rural terrain and an uninhabited rain forest. A few hours walking takes one from the center of the city into thick forest; in the process one leaves the urban sounds of street shouting and steelbands and approaches the sometimes sweet, sometimes harsh voices of monkeys, parrots and cicadas.

Port-of-Spain is a potpourri of styles, a melange of influences still mingling to form what seems like a chaotic, but for me at least, a very appealing hodgepodge. Though the most recent influences on the growth of the city and the form it has taken are British and American, previous periods of French and Spanish colonization have left their mark. From the Spanish, Port-of-Spain derives much of its orderliness, as in the grid arrangement of streets and squares in the city's center; from the French come many of its architectural motifs, especially the metal filigree ornamentation of facades, similar in some respects to that of New Orleans, a city which, arguably, is more Caribbean than North American in its style and appearance. The English have left the stamp of their stateliness in public architecture, as well as their devotion to quaintly serene parks and nooks. Much of the commerical feel of downtown Port-of-Spain imitates North American models, and this should come as no surprise since North American money and ideas are largely responsible for the new look of a commercial downtown. East Indians, though normally thought of as a resolutely rural people, have affected the city's look as well, and the rural East Indian motif of raising buildings on concrete stilts has made its way into the city. All of this has been cooked up in a Creole pot and what emerges as distinctive is not the sharp juxtaposition of a number of different stylistic influences thrown at each other, but rather the manner in which they have come together to form a somewhat haphazard but ultimately harmonious appearance. That, at least, is my impression.

Port-of-Spain is a nucleated city: there tends to be a concentration around a single center and a general orientation of structures and activities toward that center. There are no quarters or barrios, each with its own center. It is a sprawling city with relatively few multistoried buildings, though this pattern is changing in at least two very different ways: the construction of public, low-income project housing, as well as a recent proliferation of multistoried luxury apartment buildings in the more chic sections of town.

Much of the city's space is taken up with the Queen's Park Savannah (more popularly known as simply "The Savannah"), a large park in the center which contains a racetrack and numerous athletic fields, and which merges with the botanical gardens extending to the city's northern edge. The Savannah is a true city center. Everyone goes there; some are hooked on it as an arena of continually appealing activity and spend most of their time there, like the perennial hangers-on at London's Hyde Park. The Savannah's interior is turned over to sports, wandering, nighttime lovemaking. Its circumference is where most publicly available action unfolds. The thing to do for many Port-of-Spainers, particularly on a Sunday, is to walk around the Savannah or to "lime," or hang out, somewhere along its circumference and peruse the inevitably rich medley of sights and action visible from this point. The Savannah is the site of most large-scale public events: Carnival activities and other festivals, performances by black musicians; political rallies and demonstrations. Groups of musicians gather around the Savannah to rehearse and perform. Schizophrenics come here to be left alone. Children come to play. During the day countless East Indian vendors sell *roti* and other Indian delicacies from small shack-like shops and stands, while black women peddle fruit, nuts, cakes and flavored ices. At night these vendors are replaced by flambeau-lit oyster and coconut carts. At night, too, prostitutes take up their stands around the Savannah, waiting patiently for cruisers who eagerly seek them out to enjoy the anonymity of their services and pleasures in the damp grass of the Savannah.

Throughout the flatter parts of Port-of-Spain there are numerous public squares, some large and well known, others small, quiet niches in out-of-the-way neighborhoods. The availability of the square as a gathering place and as a location from which to monitor the flow of action is a key feature of the city's social ambience. The most important of these squares is Woodford Square, named after a nineteenth-century British governor (most squares are named after British governors and military heroes). Located in the very center of the business district, it is surrounded by government buildings and, on one side, by the cathedral. Woodford Square is famous in recent Trinidadian history as a center for political action and ideological expression. It is here that the People's National Movement, the majority political party, held its first large public meetings and where Dr. Eric Williams, a history professor and brilliant political orator and strategist, riveted the attention of a spellbound Trinidadian public with his lectures on Trinidad's history and his designs for Trinidad's future. In the process, he consolidated his role as a nationalist symbol and a political wizard. Williams referred to this rallying arena as the "University of Woodford Square" and he was certainly its most outstanding lecturer. He brought a politically attuned sophistication to Port-of-Spain's proletariat, whose prior exposure to education had amounted to little more than an assortment of trivial British homilies. It has been claimed, with some justification, that modern Trinidad became politicized in Woodford Square.

More recently Woodford Square has been the sight of antigovernment political rallies and, ironically, has become the arena where Williams as Prime Minister and the PNM have been most severely denounced. The promises of the "University" did not come to fruition and it is in Woodford Square where criticism and resentment have been most compellingly expressed and articulated. Antigovernment groups made Woodford Square their home in the 1960s and early 1970s, and when their rallies spilled over into the streets, creating what Trinidad's elite claimed to be a "crisis" of national internal security, the square was closed and remained off limits for more than six months. This action stunned nearly everyone since Woodford Square had always been a place where all sorts of things (and certainly all sorts of talk) had been freely permitted. Outrageous behavior was usually more tolerated here than elsewhere and deportment which would bring a frown or a scolding from mainstream enforcers anywhere else tended to be overlooked in Woodford Square. Many of the Square's habitues lived there, sleeping on its benches, and their lives were especially disrupted when the square was closed.

Imageability

In Kevin Lynch's terms Port-of-Spain is marked by a crisply legible "imageability" (1960:9). The composites of the cityscape are organized so that the mind easily transforms the physical design of the city into coherent images which facilitate recognition of the city's topographical features and structures, and allow for fluid and knowledgeable movement within its confines. As Lynch has forcefully argued, cities which can be cognitively mapped as coherent patterns allow and encourage the development of certain attitudes and facilities, and these come to deeply affect the manner in which residents approach movement and organize strategic action within such urban settings. Such facilities make it possible to regard the city as an arena which residents can explore and apprehend, rather than one which engulfs them in an unpredictable formlessness. Port-of-Spain, as such a setting, is marked by an abundance of visually stimulating nodes—parks, squares, buildings, intersections— as well as more generalized structural features—the arrangement of streets, the relationship between urban structure and design and its embedment in a physical topography. These features make the city a place which is relatively easy to "feel" structurally and to move around in knowingly.

The way in which residents of the city cognitively map its physical design is a matter of some importance both for the ethnographer and for the subjects of his inquiry. For the ethnographer, the problem of becoming familiar with the physical arena within which his observations take place concerns both his own knack for making new ground comfortable and knowable, and also the intrinsic features of that new ground itself, and the extent to which those features aid or hinder a coherent recognizability. This is true for subjects as well. The character of social maneuvering in any locale depends on much more than the intentions, plans and other essentially cognitive features of social actors and their aims. Intentions and plans emerge as realizable possibilities partly because people view the physical settings in which such possibilities unfold as workable arenas for experimenting with certain sorts of social engagements and strategic arrangements. This is the sort of thing that deviant entrepreneurs, some of whose operations I discuss in a later chapter, tend to understand with unusual clarity, although their understanding is implicit. For they need to develop such understandings if they are to exploit the contingencies emergent in these physical settings successfully. For example, in Port-of-Spain, marijuana traders must operate in fairly exposed settings if they are to attract clients, but since the work they do is illegal and therefore vulnerable to intrusion by a variety of interfering outsiders, they must be able to depart quickly and gracefully when word of possible interference arrives. Consequently, trading centers are established at points that are public and visible, but that allow for quick abandonment and escape when danger seems to encroach. Knowledge of the regular patterns of police cruising and of patrol car routes (as these are apt to be affected by the pattern of one-way streets) and a clear sense of just where the mazeway of alleyways which compose the interior of city blocks leads to go into decisions regarding where to set up such operations.

Neighborhoods of the City

A city's districts are categorized by its residents and it is convenient to refer to categorized sectors as neighborhoods. Neighborhoods have no strictly legal or administrative boundaries in Port-of-Spain, as they sometimes do elsewhere. Instead, a neighborhood's boundaries and extensions become the product of various demarcations that residents and others make in regard to the inclusivity of some sector tagged with a name. Neighborhoods are sometimes conveniently demarcated by physical boundaries such as rivers, sometimes by their social characteristics, sometimes on the basis of once relevant but no longer applicable boundary conditions. Some boundaries, and the neighborhoods they enclose, are only recognized by residents, some only by outsiders, some become reified as convenient enclosures by planners and urban bureaucrats. Some boundaries are manufactured by the press to suit their dramatic conveniences. For example, in New York City the neighborhood "Harlem" has differing boundaries and encloses different terrains according to a variety of viewpoints. Harlem is one thing for residents who live in one of its sections, something else for residents of another section, and yet another kind of entity for outsiders (actually several different sorts of constructs for different sorts of outsiders—residents of other parts of the city, reporters, city planners, social workers and so forth).

People utilize various criteria in drawing neighborhood boundaries. Often disagreements among these different assessments lead to serious problems, as when city planners arbitrarily choose to enclose some territory within the bounds of a district they feel is suitable for enclosure, much to the chagrin, anger or amusement of the people who live there. Port-of-Spain is divided into five wards for the purposes of selecting a city council and arranging for municipal administration, but this division seems neither a useful representation for city residents, nor a relevant way for the anthropologist to slice up the sociogeographical pie. Instead, division into a system of wards is an historically residual and arbitrary way of introducing order to the process of political selection.

Such questions of inclusivity and boundary determination become especially apparent at the edges of neighborhoods where one often finds descriptive ambiguity—on the part both of residents and of analysts such as the ethnographer—regarding the inclusion of an area within a larger district. Keeping the tentative and arbitrary quality of any kind of neighborhood breakdown in mind, let me offer a brief descriptive tour of Port-of-Spain's neighborhoods using a combination of criteria felt to be relevant by residents, as well as by myself, in order to offer at least some orientation to the manner in which the city's spaces are cognitively distinguished from each other and the extent to which such distinctions illuminate differences.

Downtown Port-of-Spain, known to planners and bureaucrats as the Central Business District (CBD), is a conglomeration of commercial enterprises interspersed with slum housing, and comprises a densely packed square mile or so of diverse activities and structures. Slum housing here is not so readily visible since street facades consist of stores, hotels, restaurants, bars, nightclubs, brothels, office buildings and so forth, while it is generally only the interior of downtown blocks that are taken up with decayed housing— flats, and small, meager homes arranged around alleyways and tiny yards. This arrangement creates the illusion that downtown Port-of-Spain is nothing more than a commercial hub. But concealed behind this commercial veneer and hidden from street view are some of the shabbiest dwellings and most downtrodden people in the city. For outsiders "downtown" is merely where one shops and works, while the residential life at the core of downtown blocks remains concealed and obscured. Consequently the downtown area has not developed a focused image as a residential area, either for outsiders, who tend to be blind to it, or for insiders, who tend not to concern themselves with it. Most inhabitants of Port-of-Spain, rather, see themselves as coming from named neighborhoods, for which they claim a special character, and within which they organize neighborhood organizations and activities, especially steelbands and sports clubs—and, in the recent past, street gangs. This is not true for downtown residents. Commercial intrusion prevents residential cohesiveness and a sense of neighborhood. Instead of residential contiguity there are small residential pockets, separated from each other by clusters of commercial structures. Downtown residents suffer for this, since rarely does the government turn its attention to downtowners as it does to more integrated and socially self-conscious neighborhoods that can make some claim to political patronage or to government projects or to contributions to neighborhood improvement (a new apartment project for Morvant, a youth club for East Dry River, a sports center for Belmont). Such conditions are characteristic of many American cities, where projects are often designed and designated for named and easily definable slum neighborhoods, but where the real inner city—the downtown core whose predominant functions are commerce and administration—and its residents are sadly neglected.

A person strolling through downtown streets notices primarily stores and restaurants, but he may also note, if he looks more closely, nearly invisible entrys to alleyways. These narrow alleys are most often blocked by rusty, corrugated iron gateways, which serve as barely noticeable entrances to residential pockets. Usually there are several of these alleyways within a given downtown block, and as they extend into the center of a block they form an intricate and sometimes chaotic labyrinth of paths widening at points into small yards.

On either side of an alleyway, and surrounding the yards, are very small houses, usually consisting of no more than two or three rooms, typically constructed of wood and corrugated iron. There are also multistoried structures divided into small flats. In the yards are standpipes providing water for residents. The yards are criss-crossed by clotheslines, and at almost any time of day or night, women are washing and hanging out laundry. Many women work during the day, usually as peddlers, while taking in wash in the evening to supplement daytime incomes. It is not unusual to see several women gathered in a yard to hang their laundry at two or three o'clock in the morning. These yards become centers of a social world for many residents, particularly for women with young children. Yards are not favored by men or by adolescents as places to "lime" (congregate and scan) since they afford little exposure to street scenes. Sidewalks are much better, since here one can keep a sharp eye on the flow of action. An exception here are marijuana smokers, who tend to spend much of their time off the sidewalks and away from the visibility of the streets, instead carving out little alcoves for themselves in the alleys and yards where they can smoke and get high discreetly.

Imagine a motion picture camera filming a downtown block. It records commercial establishments interspersed with visual hints of housing within the block interiors. It films clusters of limers on the sidewalk. Passing through a gateway it scans small groups of young men smoking marijuana and staying out of the way. Entering further into the center of the yards it picks up groups of women and children talking, working and playing. All of these people are black and all are poor.

Apart from these residents of block interiors, another group of downtown residents are those down-and-out men and women who make the sidewalk itself their home. It is here that those most victimized and deteriorated members of Trinidadian society more or less "live." However, in Port-of-Spain there is no skid row of the conventional sort. Instead, sidewalk residents disperse themselves around some of the heavily-trafficked and brightly-lit downtown streets. Almost all of these down-and-out sidewalk residents are very old East Indian men and women; very few are blacks. At first this seems to go against the assumption, held by most Trinidadians as well as by social scientists who have studied them, that "East Indians take care of their own." In fact they do—and they don't. While East Indian family structure tends to be very tight and while most East Indians are linked rather intimately to their kinsmen, the problem is that they have only a limited number of kinsmen, and when they survive their relatives and grow older and more isolated they lose social shoulders to lean on. Such people are left alone, with little resiliency and no kin support, and they sometimes slide downhill into extreme poverty. Blacks, faced with poverty, old age and the shrinking family ties, tend to do better. Black people have throughout their lives become accustomed to being independent and fending for themselves, maintaining flexibility and fluidity in social attachments and residential arrangements, and consequently by the time they are old, after lifetimes of being skillful, adaptable improvisers, they are much better able to take care of themselves. Cultural arrangements exhibit themselves as strengths under some circumstances, but may emerge as weaknesses as circumstances change.

Downtown Port-of-Spain exhibits the characteristics common to most urban cores: a large daytime population and a smaller nighttime residential population; a gradual but steady flow of people out of the area (although there is some replenishment by newcomers and transients); a continuing deterioration of the residential sector; a congestion of people and vehicles; and a rapid change in building types and usage with an accompanying concentration of new construction.

East Port-of-Spain (actually the southeastern portion of the city) is the great Afro-American proletarian residential domain. It has been the source and center of power of the ruling People's National Movement since independence and, more recently, a center for harshly-expressed discontent with the PNM and its policies. Steelbands emerged here, as did the mid-fifties pattern of turf-based violent street gangs and, later, militant black nationalist organizations. It is a political and cultural center of black Trinidad. Adjacent to the downtown district, East Port-of-Spain is very hilly with steep, winding streets, in contrast to the flatter, western parts of the city which are laid out in a more regular and orderly manner. Though often viewed as a uniform slum area, East Port-of-Spain contains in reality much class and residential diversity. Many middle-class blacks continue to live here while others make the bourgeois exodus to more fashionable parts of the city. Hustlers of various sorts concentrate here since this is where they find and construct much of the action that concerns them and from which they derive their incomes. Much of the housing is humble and much of it is dilapidated, but there are quite a few impressive homes. Only a careless view would see East Port-of-Spain as nothing more than a uniformly depressed slum. Further east are Morvant and Laventille, also poor black neighborhoods, but less densely populated. Here one finds an occasional goat and many chickens in addition to the human inhabitants.

Shantytown and LaBasse are south of what is properly "east" Port-of-Spain. They are depressed, deteriorated squatter areas laid out in the marshy terrain along the Gulf of Paria. Almost all housing here is constructed of scrap wood, cardboard and old corrugated iron sheets. There is little electricity, few amenities, much hunger and distress and anger. Residents of this area carry a stigma in the eyes of other Port-of-Spainers, even by those from other slum areas. Though predominantly black, Shantytown-LaBasse contains quite a few East Indians, many of these impoverished migrants to the city. Economic life here centers around the garbage dumps, and many residents earn their living retrieving rubbish which is suitable as resalable scrap material. Outsiders think of this area as largely a refuse heap for unemployed down-and-outers. This, like most impressions the bourgeoisie have of poor people, is a distortion and serves mainly as a comforting indictment. In fact, pretty trade and commerce of various sorts are carried out within the shanty area and many residents are employed in other parts of the city; some of these even have good incomes and positions but choose, for one reason or another, to reside here.

Actually community life and community consciousness tend to be tighter and more integrated here than in many other parts of the city. William Mangin (1969), among others, has argued that community solidarity and organizational arrangements are often highly articulated in shantytowns and other squatter areas. There are small businesses such as food and machine repair shops here, and numerous craftsmen and tradesmen, including tailors, dressmakers and cobblers. Itinerant vendors cruise the area in great numbers, selling a wide assortment of items to residents who would rather make purchases close to home than go downtown. The reality, then, reveals a bustling, alive conglomeration of people and enterprises, and a never-ending display of the ingenuity which the poorest of peoples so often reveal in giving meaning to what, from the point of view of outsiders, seem to be shattered and shapeless lives.

Belmont is a large, densely populated neighborhood east of the Savannah. It is an old and very attractive area, and has for years been the base of lower middle-class and "respectable" working-class black people. The housing here tends to be more substantial than in East Port-of-Spain, the adjoining neighborhood to the south. In the past Belmont was what the "colored" bourgeoisie called home, but as the middle class made its all-too-familiar exodus to the suburbs, Belmont has become more and more a strictly black neighborhood. During the political turmoil of 1970, Belmont became a key staging area of dissent and militant action, and since the struggle for independence Belmont has remained a highly ideologized and politicized district. The National Joint Action Committee, the pivotal organization involved in the 1970 "revolt", as well as several other black nationalist and leftist organizations have had their headquarters in Belmont and continue to do so. Belmont, like East Port-of-Spain, is viewed as an especially "hip" section of the city, one in which there are varieties of intriguing action to encounter, and where a young man or woman on the move is likely to discover involving scenes.

St. Anns is a neighborhood encompassing a wide variety of residential types and social aggregates. It is not technically within the city limits but most people nevertheless think of it as part of the city. St. Anns lies at the northernmost edge of Port-of-Spain, at the base of the foothills of the Northern Range. The neighborhood is quite mixed, and contains a variety of ethnic and class segments, sometimes seeming to be a microcosm of the country as a whole. The heart of St. Anns is a valley cut through by the very unsubstantial St. Anns river. Rising steeply from the valley are a series of hills. The smaller range of hills to the east encompasses the middle-class enclave of Cascade. The much steeper hills to the north are dotted with quasi-rural squatter pockets. The big hill to the west of the valley contains the homes of many of Trinidad's economic elite. The valley itself is broken up into a number of peculiarly set-off pockets containing small, homogeneous aggregates, from upper-class European expatriates to very poor working-class black people, all arranged in a rather helter-skelter manner. The center of St. Anns is a half-hour walk from downtown and a ten-minute walk from the Savannah. But a mile north of St. Anns center one can find little villages that are nearly replicas of typical villages in Trinidad's rural, black zones, and perhaps three miles north of St. Anns center, one runs up against the beginnings of the rain forest.

For a time I myself lived in a house by the St. Anns river. Across the river from me were a cluster of homes occupied by some of Trinidad's toniest up-and-comers. Immediately adjacent to the grounds of my house were several clusters of squatter shacks. Across the river from these shacks an air-conditioned set of "luxury" flats was under construction. And behind these flats the beginnings of the Upper Hutton Road section—a very poor, black, semi-rural area—ran up a series of small hills. The ethnic and class heterogenity, while in a meaningless way conforming to the government's image of a Trinidad where "races live side by side," actually yields a neighborhood where there is virtually no interaction or rapport among class and ethnic segments. Whites here stick very closely together. So does the black and "colored" middle-class; so do the poor blacks in the hills and the shacks along the upper St. Anns river. The only real social cement (though certainly it is no cement of rapport) results from the fact that the area's poor blacks serve as a dirt-cheap labor source for the whites of the area—as their maids, gardeners, cooks and laborers.

Woodbrook and Newtown lie directly west and northwest of the central business district. The western part of the city, unlike the eastern, is quite flat and streets are laid out in an orderly gridlike pattern. This neighborhood is a mix of commercial structures and residences. As one moves east to west in Port-of-Spain, and then on to the suburbs, one takes a socioeconomic journey to increasingly bourgeois terrains. Newtown and Woodbrook are lower middle-class enclaves with some pockets of both quite poor and quite affluent residence. This is a very densely packed neighborhood, but it is the density of fairly substantial houses neatly arranged next to each other, rather than the slum density of very small, proximate, cheap and often fragile struc-tures packed on top of each other. Much of the architecture here is of the French Creole sort, with ornate metal roofs and grill work.

The ethnic and class composition of the area is complex. Woodbrook, since the middle of the past century, has been known as a stronghold of Port-of-Spain's "colored" middle class and professionals, especially civil servants. This continues to be true although there have been changes in the composi-tion of the neighborhood in recent years. With the recognition that Wood-brook and Newtown are so conveniently located vis-a-vis the banks and commercial houses of downtown, and with the growing popularity of apart-ment living, many middle-class whites are moving into recently constructed flats. The neighborhood also contains large numbers of Portuguese, Chinese, and "Syrian" residents. Syrians, actually descendents of several sorts of Middle Eastern migrants, have been taking over large sections of Woodbrook and rather intentionally establishing an ethnic niche there. Poor black people who live in this section—and there are many of them—are especially con-vinced of this, claiming that the Syrians are buying up all available property and "kicking all of we out." Black-Syrian animosity is a key motif of ethnic relations in this part of the city.

In spite of the overall bourgeois ambience there is a good deal of interior-block slum housing here, similar to that which characterizes downtown. In the midst of otherwise crisp and tidy middle-class blocks there are often small yards containing shacks which house poor black residents. These are the source of some continuing tension, as the bourgeois sensibilities of many neighborhood dwellers are offended by this proletarian intrusion. Such offense has not been effectively transformed into political pressure, much to the chagrin of "respectable" residents, as the government continues to stay away from what it knows would be politically inexpedient intervention.

Although Woodbrook and Newtown have the feel of quintessentially stable, respectable neighborhoods—perhaps the most orderly and staid in all of the city—these neighborhoods house more "hustling clubs" (casinos and whorehouses) than any other section of town. There are several reasons for this. The most compelling is that middle-class men like to play and they prefer having their places of entertainment nearby. This middle-class clientele of "sin" is not likely to cruise for its action in East Port-of-Spain with its very nitty-gritty sorts of clubs. Effective police payoffs may be another reason: for there seems to be particularly good rapport between the area's club owners and the local police. Furthermore, the low-keyed tone of this neighborhood provides the right kind of ambience for the discretion which whoring and gambling seem to require.

St. Clair is Port-of-Spain's one truly posh neighborhood. It borders the Savannah on the east. The cream of Trinidad's elite live here. Each house is an expensive, spacious unit insulated and isolated from others. There is no feeling of neighborhood at all, for the rich prefer private, protected worlds to public, socially fluid settings. The key to the ambience are the many well-trained guard and attack dogs who zealously protect these rarefied enclosures and harass black children who choose to take an adventurous walk on the other side of the tracks.

At the eastern edge of St. Clair and bordering the Savannah is Maraval Road—Port-of-Spain's fantasy street and major tourist attraction. Stretched out along its length are a number of pseudo-chateaux, some in Florentine, some in Gothic, some in Rococco styles. Some are merely extravagantly baroque and eclectic. One of these buildings is the Prime Minister's office. Another is the residence of the archbishop. Some are the "ancestral" homes (though the time-depth is very shallow) of a few of Trinidad's wealthiest ersatz-baronial families. The largest is Queen's Royal College, the most prestigious of Port-of-Spain's secondary schools and the alma mater of Eric Williams and many other illustrious Trinidadians.

Further west lies St. James, where nearly all of Port-of-Spain's East Indians have lived for several decades. St. James is one of the city's liveliest neighborhoods. One can find as much nightlife here as anywhere in Trinidad, and this is the only section of the city where the action is lively and where restaurants, food stores and snackettes are open very late at night. Going out after the bars close in Port-of-Spain almost always means a trip to St. James for a *roti* at an East Indian spot, or fried chicken at the Royal Castle. St. James has the rich, full feel of the city—dense and congested, busy and commerical, lively and rewarding to the adventurer. The Indians who live here are nearly all wage earners, or shop and small business owners. And one sees a marked contrast between the traditional "country" Indians who have recently migrated here, and urban, Creole Indians who have lived here for many years and who tend to look down their cosmopolitan noses at their country-bumpkin cousins.

The architecture of St. James has a rural East Indian influence and many of the houses—and all those built by Indians—are constructed on concrete stilts. In rural areas homes built on such stilts provide room underneath the house for livestock shelters and kitchens, as well as cool, shady places for large East Indian families to congregate. In the city this feature remains, but without its traditional function; the motif has become an identifying mark of an East Indian residence. St. James is dotted with the prayer flags usually found standing in front of Hindu homes. The entire St. James area has a reputation, held by outsiders and especially by blacks, as an arena of crime and violence. For the most part this assessment is no more than an extension of the indictment most non-Indians make of Indians as a violent people. Nevertheless, organized crime does flourish here, linked to the control of illegal enterprises and business monopolies, and there have been some machine gun-enlivened "wars" among East Indian rivals.

The Suburbs

The suburbs of Port-of-Spain range east and west of the city for the most part; northward expansion has been limited by the rugged terrain. In recent years suburban growth has been just as rapid and stunning a development as it has been for North American cities. Many suburban districts have only been built up recently, expanding into uninhabited terrain or replacing unproductive rural enclaves unable to resist suburban intrusion and all the wily machinations of the developers. The suburbs are increasingly taking on a North American style and appearance, complete with all the forgettable accoutrements which accompany rapid suburban growth. This has been especially true of the suburbs west of the city, of which Diego Martin is typical.

Diego Martin is a sprawling, amorphous stretch of scattered and newly developed suburban pockets. It is very much the suburb to move to for the upwardly mobile middle-classes of Port-of-Spain, foremost among them civil servants. Some sections, such as Diamond Vale, are large tract developments of endlessly replicated identical houses and streets arranged in a neat, orderly, sterile pattern. Other enclaves are distinguished from each other in various ways—by residents' income levels, ethnicity, architectural style. Interspersed among all the middle-class housing are squatter pockets. This whole region was very much a squatter area before the developers moved in, and while the developers have been thorough and efficient in altering the face of the Diego Martin region, many squatters remain, tenaciously sticking with their little holdings and coolly resisting the frustrated attempts to evict them quickly and smoothly. This is one of the juxtapositions of modern Trinidad: squeezed in among what otherwise would be (much to the dismay of the city's respectable escapees) a uniformly bourgeois preserve, live clusters of squatters who grow their crops on tiny tracts of unpopulated land, usually a few miles from where they reside—modern and traditional Trinidad living cheek by jowl. In Diego Martin we see another modern suburban phenomenon: the traffic jam. Movement into this area has accelerated dramatically in recent years and with this the automobile has made its impact. However, there has been little additional road building, and particularly during the rainy season, when there is much flooding in this section of the country, the whole area succumbs to a partial paralysis.

The eastern suburbs of Port-of-Spain, stretched out along the Eastern Main Road, are very different in character. Partly this is a matter of topography. West of the city the terrain is hilly, while going east it becomes flat.

Consequently, while development of the western suburbs has been a planned and determined effort, the eastern suburbs have expanded by sprawl—the expansion of city lifestyles to areas adjacent to the city. This sprawl has followed the extension of industry into areas directly east of the city. The eastern suburbs are much more proletarian in tone and composition than those to the west. They elaborate on the typical urban patterns of residence, work and social style, unlike the western suburbs, which are the results of conscientious efforts to imitate North American suburban models. The suburban towns along the Eastern Main Road all mix industry, commerce and residence. Access from Port-of-Spain to most of the rest of the country requires passing through these suburbs and consequently there is quite a bit of traffic through the area, stimulating commercial development of all sorts, particularly of enterprises related to automobile sales and servicing. This, combined with increased factory construction and opportunities for blue-collar employment, has imparted to the area a largely industrial, proletarian character. Furthermore, while the western suburbs are populated almost exclusively by those of European and African ancestry (as well as by a substantial number of Americans employed as technicians and professionals), more than half of the residents of the eastern suburbs are East Indians. Just south of this suburban stretch lies Caroni County, the heart of Trinidad's East Indian social world. Rural Indians, migrating to the city, have tended recently to settle in the city's eastern suburbs, in close proximity to their rural origins, rather than moving to the city itself. So with both an inflow of rural East Indians, and an outflow of residents from the city itself, the suburban zone east of the city is Trinidad's most rapidly growing region.

Ethnicity and Class in the City

In rural Trinidad, districts tend to be ethnically homogeneous. One can travel through most of the villages of Caroni County and imagine himself in India. A person traveling only forty miles or so from Port-of-Spain to the northeastern corner of the island (where Herskovits studied "Africanisms"), encounters a nearly exclusively Afro-Caribbean social domain. A resident of Caroni may not encounter a black man or woman for weeks. A black farmer from a Northern Range village hears all sorts of things about East Indians but rarely runs across one. In the city, these social and cultural distances are dramatically reduced. Residential proximity, the concentration of a polyethnic population in a limited area, and social fluidity mean that residents routinely encounter and scan, at close range, the behaviors and styles of members of ethnic groups other than their own. This is a paramount feature of the urban scene in Port-of-Spain. From such conditions emerge the multifaceted ethnic disclosures, encounters and assessments which make up so much of the ambience of the city. The visibility of a wide variety of "different" behavior and display is a key ingredient of the culture of the city.

The ethnographer is disposed to make two contrasting guesses about what such a situation of interethnic proximity may imply. The first hypothesis proposes fear, prejudice and hostility as characteristic of a social setting where the indicted outsider ("nigger," "coolie," "honky," "chinee creole") is not present, not available for direct scrutiny, and where, consequently, myths about the outsider may be easily sustained since they are never subject to the critique of direct evidence and disclosure. It certainly seemed to me, for example, that rural East Indians continued to hold a range of outrageously distorted beliefs about blacks, while urban East Indians, forced to directly encounter the blacks among them and to consider the inconsistencies between their old myths and a now available reality, softened or abandoned their harsh views of blacks.

The other guess is that the tight, proximate interactive basis of urban social relations is likely to increase friction and tension. Myths held at a distance may remain casual indictments with little power and few effects on actual behavior. It's just a matter of sitting around in your village and bad-mouthing the "others" who live far away. But in a city, *lives* are actually brought into proximity with each other. It is no longer merely myths that clash, but people, and henceforth ethnic antagonisms in the city may become explosive. There is certainly dramatic evidence to support this view, though much less from Port-of-Spain than, for example, from Boston.

Both guesses may end up being accurate assessments of differing inter-ethnic situations and conditions. What may generally be claimed is that the contours of urban life, particularly the immediacy and directness of personal experience and the opportunity to scan a wide variety of stylistic possibilities, generate certain sorts of tensions, adjustments, compromises and value shifts. Familiarity may lead at once to a greater ease in dealing with categorically "distant" people, while exposing and exaggerating conflicts that in more parochial, less cosmopolitan settings are more sublimated and less clarified.

Rural Trinidad is largely carved up out of ethnic territories where those of a particular ethnic background live among their own. In the city, residents of different ethnic backgrounds tend to live side by side, and pockets of residence are never far from other such pockets. Some Port-of-Spain neighborhoods have evolved in such a way that social relations among the very different kinds of people inside them are extensive and harmonious. Often interpersonal and intergroup relations extend across classes but not across ethnic lines, while sometimes the opposite is true. In Diego Martin class-based commitments and styles bring together a bourgeoisie of many different shades. In St. James "Indianness" counts much more than class position in establishing rapport and acceptance. Such diverse arrangements have different implications for the manner in which social relations within and across ethnic segments are conducted. These implications will emerge in the description of social settings and occasions in the following chapters.

Pluralism and Creolization in the City

One may look across the social landscape of Trinidad and distill two very different, though equally informed, impressions. The first impression is one of dispersion of separable sociocultural elements across the society—a spectrum of ethnic groupings—as centrally descriptive of social reality; this is the pluralist view. The second impression is of an homogenizing process whereby the culturally disparate components of the society become more and more similar over time, tending to fuse in the formation of a national culture: this is the creolist view. These two perspectives convey distinctive ideological overtones as well. Optimists—the government and the seekers of consensus— see Trinidadian social history moving along a vector from pluralism to a creolized unification. Such a view claims that though Trinidad started off, and for two centuries continued to develop, as a society of markedly contrasted and separable groups—African slaves, European migrants, a "colored" bourgeosie, East Indians, Chinese—in recent years the trend has been toward a lessening of the significance of ethnic differences and the consolidation of a national, Trinidadian culture. Critics, skeptics and cynics see an altogether different picture. They continue to notice, as most distinctive, the entrenched divisiveness of the country's social and ethnic segments. Unimpressed by public relations visions of consensus and harmony, they view Trinidad as fixed in patterns of class and ethnic differences and antagonisms.

But one sees both creolization and pluralism in the city. The picture looks something like this: groups which in rural Trinidad were demographically separable found themselves in contact with each other in the city and this affected both inter-ethnic styles of behavioral encounters as well as the constellation of values, often racist ones, that animate such encounters. To some extent creolization, the emergence of a national cultural style, has in fact occurred. But creolization has not meant the symbiotic or compatible rapport or fusion of the two "primary" cultures—black and East Indian—but, rather, what may be called the "Negrofication" of the East Indian, as well as the Americanization of both. That is, a Creole cultural style has been developing all along but it has excluded East Indian elements almost entirely. The East Indian in Trinidad becomes a cultural loser when he moves to a setting where correspondence between cultural plans and social realities becomes no longer possible, when conditions no longer make it feasible or practical to live life according to a design developed to suit very different sorts of circumstances. The city is such a setting. East Indian cultural intentions have been most fully realized in rural, ethnically homogeneous environments. Movement to the city and away from such compatible conditions, has made it increasingly difficult for urban East Indians to maintain the integrity of their rural cultural styles. The city, with its overwhelming Afro-American tone, provides an arena where East Indians find it difficult to sustain traditional behavioral patterns, or where they choose not to. In the city Indians face pressures to modify their behavior to conform to the urban model—the creolized version of a Trinidadian culture. In short, a kind of creolization has occurred. Traditional Creole styles (which exclude such elements as the East Indian) have combined with what may be called modern industrial culture, in association with various Americanisms, to yield a distinctive cultural amalgam. This amalgam cannot be described exhaustively, but I will illustrate some of its facets in the following chapters.

Caribbean anthropology has focused overwhelmingly on rural peoples and settings, reflecting the habits of anthropologists more than the real punctuations of the *modern* West Indian scene. No longer can we learn too much about Caribbean society and culture as a whole by studying selected villages and hamlets. Cosmopolitanism has spread its flavors and effects. This is certainly true of Trinidad and, I suspect, it is becoming increasingly true of many Caribbean societies.

Chapter 3

Style and Adaptation in a Depressed Urban Setting

I refer to the setting as depressed, and by this I mean something rather different from—and simpler than—most attributions of this feature to a social setting. For me, claiming that a people or a locale is depressed is to say that it is poor; it is a sector characterized by a scarcity of resources relative to other sectors of the wider society of which it is a part. I do not mean, however, socially or culturally depressed, for such a description often serves as an indictment of a group or a population. Descriptions of peoples as being socially or culturally deficient have tended to become judgments about what amounts to the good life, and such judgments have lent a distinctive flavor to much of the writing about the lifestyles of the poor. The analysis of Afro-American societies has been deeply flawed by the intrusion of seemingly liberal ideologies claiming to know all about why and how some social segment has become damaged but, being ideologies, turn away from a naturalistic description of such purportedly damaged sections. The most common question about Afro-American life has *not* been, "What is Afro-American social experience like in all its detail?", but, "Have Afro-Americans become damaged because they adhere to an unhealthy culture or because they live in an unhealthy environment?" It is within the confines of this latter question that much of the debate concerning black Americans has been conducted. But if we start from the assumption that a population's adaptations are unhealthy, we can make very little headway in understanding the experiences which shape that population's flow of everyday life. As anthropologists, this is what we should always be after: what that life looks like and how it has been shaped.

In this chapter I wish to put forth a series of portraits and vignettes that may provide glimpses of the flow of life among young black men in Port-of-Spain. Too often we assume that what we are about to study as social scientists will have a structure that tends to be cohesive and that we can describe as a system. But everyday experience belies such analytical optimism. Life is messy, disorderly, fleeting, fragmented, amorphous, evanescent. Society is an assortment of variously collected social minutiae that we cannot easily group under an umbrella of systematic understanding. Social scientists instinctively and defensively reject such a recognition, and instead often attempt too orderly a description of society. Journalists, also concerned with describing social life, relish the minutiæ, the complexity, the labyrinthine confusion of social life. And while social science has derived much of its analytical power just because it has looked for structure and system and here and there discovered regularities, journalism finds much of its own strength in the freedom to explore activity and experience unbounded by overly complex and encapsulating categories. Journalistic illumination, when it is good, derives its insights through cues offered by the discourse of everyday life. Social science tends to create special languages very different from daily languages or "emic" representations. Sometimes the use of such special languages aids in illumination, sometimes it distorts, conceals and obscures. I feel there is much to be said for following journalistic style and approaching social description by using ordinary members' terms and concepts when these seem approrpiate.

Years ago Erving Goffman claimed that a most proper, though often neglected, arena for social investigation is the texture of everyday life experiences; not social structure, but personal experience as it is socially shaped. While "great" events such as initiation, marriage, death, accession to status punctuate the flow of everyday life, the space between such punctuations comprises the bulk of experience: the endless progression of twenty-four-hour days. Understanding everyday life experiences requires describing social behavior in such a way as to reveal its *strategy* and its *style* from the point of view of conscious and purposeful designs of persons engaged in activity, and by considering the ordinary idiom which members of a society use to refer to their styles and strategies. While we can use the word *action* in its Weberian-Parsonian sense to refer to patterns of culturally based and socially located behavior by groups of people who share models "of" and "for" orientation, in everyday speech this word–action points to an ambience of energy and directedness that is sought and created. Goffman took this ordinary-language notion of action as the pivot for his famous essay, "Where the action is" (1967:149 ff). Goffman views action as something people looked for or looked to avoid, as something they worked to create or worked to diffuse. He wishes to find out exactly what engaged people consider to be "action," and how they go about finding it or making it come their way. My approach in this book is similar in that I want to draw the outlines of a landscape of social experience that I shared with my informants during my stay in Trinidad and in this way to illuminate part of the social experiences of black men in Port-of-Spain: this book, therefore, is actor-centered.

What I wish to disclose are matters of *style*. Style is elusive, multifaceted, slippery. It is best revealed through illustrations and examples rather than via systematically constructed models. By providing brief portraits of flesh and blood people (though names and some details have been changed to protect the innocent and the guilty), and describing the sorts of scenes engaging their attention and their commitment, as well as the settings which they inhabit, I hope to give the reader some sense of what this urban, Trinidadian cultural ambience is like.

It is difficult to defend my choice of informants. Such a choice results partly from fortuitous encounters. Some of these encounters seemed fruitful in that I gained the sense that focusing on certain people and participating in the flow of their lives and their scenes would, first, be achievable and, furthermore, allow some intimate entry to what, for me at least, seemed an interesting world. Ethnography in a field as complex and seemingly chaotic as a modern city often means looking around, approaching and participating where you can, attaching oneself to settings in an accommodating and minimally obtrusive way, and sometimes behaving like a remora hooked to the belly of a shark: clinging closely and sucking in experience vicariously. I hoped that the small number of people with whom I spent extensive time, and the particular worlds they revealed to me, would prove representative of something larger. But I recognized the difficulty here. The search for typicality usually proves futile. Life surprises us with its diversity and its disorder more often than with its generalities and consistencies. This is not a scientific claim but a metaphysical one. The construction of the typical is a homogenizing process that takes place in the analyst's head as he seeks to weave a usually dazzling array of impressions into a unified image (system, model, structure, pattern, gestalt). As such, the claim of typicality and neat order always exists in tension with disorderly social reality.

Hence the description in this chapter of a group of men and their lives does not claim to be microcosmic; it is not urban Trinidad in miniature that I wish to describe. Rather, I aim for an illustrative description, one that informs about *some* general aspects of the lives of the urban poor in a West Indian city. The "some" needs to be emphasized. Every ethnographer eventually gains useful access to certain sorts of scenes while finding himself almost completely closed off from others. The most significant fact here is the gender of the investigator. In a world composed of smaller worlds of men and women, being a man or a woman often determines accessibility and, ultimately, reliability as well. Other relevant factors affecting ethnographic accessibility include the investigator's temperament, interests, luck, patience and age. All these factors taken together tend to position the ethnographer at some vantage point from which he makes his observations. A further absolutely essential, though obvious, implication is that he is absent from other points where he could gain other impressions.

Characters

CARL WINSTON ("CRYSTAL")

Carl Winston was born and spent most of his childhood in San Fernando, a town in southern Trinidad. He moved to Port-of-Spain in 1963 and lived there until emigrating to Canada in 1971. While I knew him, Carl saw himself as a Port-of-Spainer, as someone "from town," and no longer as someone "from south." In a society where Port-of-Spain is the epitome of sophistication and street savvy while the rest of the country is seen as lagging behind, this distinction becomes important as an ingredient of one's identity. While he lived in San Fernando, Carl had a common-law wife and, with her, two children. His ex-wife now lives in New York City and the children live with their maternal grandmother in San Fernando. Occasionally Carl stopped by to see his children and seemed to be a warm and tender father, but his fatherly commitments were very limited; he provided no financial support, and none was expected from him. Altogether, he was quite detached from anything that resembled family life.

As a boy of thirteen Carl began to work as an occasional laborer at the Texaco docking facilities in the refinery town of Pointe-a-Pierre. He spent a number of years working for Texaco but felt stranded there, never doing much besides tedious manual labor. He left Texaco and began working for the Singer Sewing Machine Company in San Fernando, first as a handyman, then as retail clerk, and finally as a traveling salesman complete with company car. Carl claimed (and others corroborated) that he was doing very well at Singer, on his way to joining their central sales staff. But one day he decided to take out a "loan" from Singer, removing some cash from the office with the intention, so he claimed, of returning it promptly. But he was caught and the infraction cost him his job. The need for this loan, like so many of Carl's financial needs, stemmed from his involvement in gambling, particularly betting on the horses. After this incident Carl decided to leave San Fernando and to try his luck in Port-of-Spain. By the time of his move Carl had already gained quite a reputation as a steelbandsman and man-about-town. But he abandoned his accomplishments and his status and decided to head out for the big time.

Carl had no family in Port-of-Spain and lived by himself in a rooming house. But he did have a number of close friends who had preceded him from San Fernando. He began working as a cab driver, taking over another man's taxi for a few hours each day. He did this, he said, because it afforded the perfect opportunity to earn at least some sort of a living while learning what the city was all about. Taxi drivers become connoisseurs of the city's streets and Carl was the sort of man who wanted to understand the nuances of his environment as quickly as possible. But the nickel-and-dime income of part-time cab driving was insufficient, particularly as Carl was beginning to lead a rather flashy and costly style of life in Port-of-Spain. He managed to get a job with Singer in Port-of-Spain—his previous transgression with the company was forgiven—and worked at this for a while. But tedium took over while a hunger to become a car salesman increased. Cars had always fascinated Carl, as they do most young Trinidadian males. One would imagine the automobile to be a rather peripheral concern for the poor in a Third World society such as Trinidad. But in Trinidad the "route taxi," cabs which run regular routes through the city and throughout the country, picking up and discharging passengers along the route, and charging a small, fixed fee, are the major mode of public transport. Hence many Trinidadians own cars and use these regularly or sporadically as taxicabs. The automobile then becomes an instrument of work enabling many Trinidadians to own cars who under other circumstances could not dream of such a thing.

Carl loved automobiles, had sales exprience at Singer, felt self-confident and knew he was persuasive in his dealings with people, and so he began to regard car sales as the perfect sort of work for himself. He got a job with one of Port-of-Spain's largest used car dealers, and for five years he continued at this line of work, affiliated with three large and reputable car dealerships. Carl made rather good money selling used cars. Commission sales appealed to him, dovetailing with his ability to sell and with the excellent rapport he was usually able to develop with clients. As a salesman Carl had himself a "bourgeois" income and this, together with the continuous availability of a car (he never bothered or needed to own one of his own) allowed Carl to lead the sort of life he wanted: a bachelor's life revolving around action or, as he put it, "kicks," especially the kicks of gambling and, as they say in Trinidad, "womanizing."

During my stay in Trinidad, Carl's financial world began to fall apart as gambling pressures mounted. He was also beginning to have trouble at work. This had nothing to do with his competence as a salesman, but with his boss's disapproval of his friends and his personal style. His employers felt that for a man in his position, earning his kind of income, a continued commitment to the street life of ghetto blacks and hustlers was inappropriate. Two separate incidents finally caused Carl to lose his last job as a car salesman: he promised to sell a car to a customer without clearing it with the company, a minor transgression which the company chose to make much of; and, more seriously, he allowed a disreputable and rather roguish friend to borrow a company car he himself had been using, and the friend smashed it up.

Carl lost his job but was not initially too unhappy. He claimed that salesmanship had begun to lose much of the allure it originally held for him. He no longer felt comfortable with the pressure of having to persuade clients to make purchases. He disliked the snobbish ways of his employers and of the "bourgeois"[3] salesmen he worked with, who felt only contempt for the poor blacks of the eastern sections of Port-of-Spain, the sector most of Carl's friends came from. He was tired of the routine of daily work and the way in which it increasingly polarized his life into the spheres of bourgeois money-making respectability, and the street world's action and allure. He viewed himself as a hustler already, since he saw car sales as a hustling profession. And he felt he would try a more appealing mode of hustling-as-work, one more in tune with his preferred scenes and styles: distributing and selling marijuana. Many of his friends had illegal hustles of one sort or another and some of them were doing quite well, or at least well enough to get along in a manner compatible with their limited needs. But after years of making good money, Carl's tastes had become rather expensive and he was not prepared for the drastic drop in income he experienced when he stopped selling cars and began selling marijuana. Carl, who for many years had been a conventionally employed man, was becoming deviant. He was caught in a bind and he began to walk a tightrope. Fond of the money he made as a salesman, and somewhat less fond of the status and style which went with this bourgeois sort of work; attracted to the freedom and flexibility hustling made possible and the unpretentious ambience of the streets, but unprepared for such a marked drop in his income, Carl really couldn't make it. Once he was completely inside the hustling life he realized it was not quite so easy nor so consistently pleasant. Instead, new troubles and pressures presented themselves. He could no longer meet his well developed and long cultivated financial needs. He failed as a marijuana trader; his money began to run out; he had difficulty meeting his rent payments; and finally, after being caught up in some serious trouble involving a possible criminal indictment, he decided to leave Trinidad, feeling caught in a morass of social and financial traps. In July, 1971 Carl and his friend Derek moved to Montreal.

Carl was a rather well-known man about town, partly because of his access to cars and his easy mobility. He was an unusually personable man, with a low-keyed, but very sharp and witty style—the sort very much appreciated in Trinidad. He was quite handsome, had light and what Trinidadians call "Spanish" skin, a sharp, hawkish nose, a big Zapata-style mustache, and deep, alert eyes. He was a very smooth womanizer, gentle and patient with women, with little of the gruff, demanding, "come here woman," stud-like style so typical of many Trinidadian men. He did very well in his many liaisons with women. He had a detailed, up-to-date knowledge of Port-of-Spain and the range of scenes that were continually unfolding in the city. He had numerous contacts and easy rapport among Indians and other non-blacks. Even more than most Trinidadians, who make it a point to be knowledgeable about music, Carl had a sophisticated and current knowledge of musical trends and developments. Among some of the city's circles he had become known as

"Crystal," his monicker. Nearly all Trinidadian men, even among the bourgeoisie, have nicknames or monickers. The Crystal of the streets of East Dry River and Carl Winston the automobile salesman in a sense occupied two different worlds, which sometimes converged and overlapped. This turned out to be Carl's crucial problem: juggling his lifestyles and associations to maintain some harmony, freedom, and serenity while continuing to remain on top of things. For much of my stay in Trinidad, Carl seemed to succeed, moving back and forth among very different sorts of scenes, stylizing his stances and maneuvers as he went along, but ultimately he failed. Born poor, a quintessentially Caribbean proletarian man, bourgeois successes elevated his expectations and his tastes. But the intimacy, familiarity, down-to-earth excitement and street-based rapport of a poorer, more basic and essential world continued to hold a grip on him. Ultimately this grip was stronger than the allure of respectability and success. But, spoiled by success and pressured by bourgeois expectations, Carl lost much of his resiliency. And when he tried to turn once again to the street world, his efforts were tarnished by a struggle to readapt. Carl's life and styles are illustrative of a most typical Caribbean syndrome: the disharmony between what is viewed as "roots"—loyalty to the streets and to one's background, especially one's blackness, and the alluring possibility of modern bourgeois success and achievement.

DEREK HARRIS ("RASTAMAN")

Derek had been Carl's closest friend since their childhood in San Fernando. They are still together, having jointly ventured a move to Montreal in order to give their fortunes a chance in North America. Derek was very dark and unusual in appearance. He wore his hair in dreadlocks, the permanent braids of the Rastafarian cultists of Jamaica. Derek became enchanted with the Rastas a few years before I met him, after having befriended several Rasta brethren on a trip to Jamaica. With Derek's compelling presence and influence, several of his younger proteges began to wear their hair in Rasta fashion as well and to profess commitment to Rastafarian ideals and beliefs.

Derek came from a "respectable" working-class family. By the time he was a teenager, his father, originally a carpenter, had become a small-time contractor with a few men occasionally in his employ. With his climb to this limited success, the father tried to bring Derek, the oldest of several children, along on the journey to bourgeois respectability. But Derek rebelled and spurned his family's new found successes and ideals. Although his assessment of the past, including the dynamics of his own upbringing, was no doubt colored by his new absorption with Rastafarian interpretations of history and society, I got the impression that Derek had been a rebel from early years and that his restless search for a unified worldview, linked to a distaste for his family's new "social" concerns, predisposed him to the Rasta message in the first place. Derek claimed that even when he was quite young he recognized that his parents' pretensions were a sham. He turned away from his family as an adolescent and they, in turn, spurned him. His father permitted Derek to remain in the house and take his meals there through his teenage years but, sensing that Derek was "bad," his parents attempted to deflect his influence from his brothers and sisters, unwilling to have his "rude" ways taint their other children.

While still in San Fernando Derek began to get involved in petty criminal escapades, though only peripherally. He visited gambling spots and illegal cockfights; he accompanied others in their small-time larcenies; he transported illegal bush rum ("mountain dew"). Derek was a bit younger than Carl and as a youth had been very much influenced by him, and so when Carl began to gain some stability with his Singer sales job, he tried to push Derek in the same direction, and convinced Singer to hire Derek in spite of what had turned into, by this time, a nasty reputation as troublemaker. Derek did menial and what he felt was degrading work at Singer (He was the clean-up and errand boy, the "boy" who is always around commercial enterprises and who is expected to hop and jump at the bidding of the more secure and respectable employees). This didn't sit very well with Derek, and, irritated by the tedium and the petty humiliations tossed his way, he quit his job at Singer. Through a friend of his father's Derek obtained work as a contractor's assistant and over the course of a year or two became a good carpenter, though he continued to be paid very poorly by his standards. But with a building boom in San Fernando during the early 1960s, Derek's skills as a carpenter became very much more in demand, and he worked for several contractors and was beginning to make some money and was considering carpentry as a trade. But soon after Carl and several other friends moved to Port-of-Spain, Derek too began to feel impelled to leave. His last job down south involved working as a carpenter on the construction of luxury homes for Texaco executives. He didn't care for this.

In Port-of-Spain Derek drifted in a very different direction than Carl. Carl came to the city to try to make it economically and to "rise" in the world; Derek came trying to find some sort of consistency in his social circumstances to overcome a sense of his family's failures and hypocrisies, and to seek new sorts of "action" as well. Derek quickly gravitated toward East Port-of-Spain, the center of black and "youth"[5] consciousness and a world of hustle as well. While Carl divided his life between the shirt-and-tie style of the car lot and the nitty-gritty of the streets, Derek became completely absorbed by the strategic, action-charged world of the streets, and soon became a prime exponent of that world. Physically tough, smart, always alert to the nuances of practical circumstances and shifts in the social wind, and possessed of a surplus of savvy as well, Derek fit in quite nicely in Port-of-Spain's action-oriented street world. He became an East Port-of-Spain hustler par excellence—a man who acquires part or all of his income through inventive maneuvers, many of them illegal, rather than through conventional employment.

Derek had little interest in conventional socioeconomic success and stability, which he considered prosaic, undesirable, and, in any case, not open to him. He was wary of the mainstream culture, the European-derived baggage of what he viewed to be an assortment of deceits. Although Derek did not involve himself actively in radical or black nationalist politics, he shared with those actively committed to such politics a cynicism regarding the bourgeois aspirations of the "total" society as these aspirations were spelled out by its cultural brokers and power holders. He maintained a tough, rebellious style of approach and engagement that brought him into continuous conflict with established institutional powers. The toughness, cynicism and fatalism combined for a while to propel Derek to serious crime—burglary and robbery. For a few years he acquired a reputation as a rough though petty hoodlum. Such a reputation only increased his difficulties, bringing him into continual conflict with others, and some of these conflicts came close to costing Derek his life. He entered the world of "bad johns"—active, violent criminals who placed a premium on toughness and command. This was one end of East Port-of-Spain's hustling world, but one that many were beginning to repudiate in the 1960s.

The close calls he faced over and over again eventually affected Derek: he began smoking more marijuana and his interests turned to cultural movements such as pan-Africanism and the Jamaica Rastafari. Having lived out his rebellion in violence and challenge for a few years, Derek now turned to contemplation and reflection. As he began to affiliate himself more and more closely with a milieu which centered around getting high on marijuana (in the late 1960s this was still a rather limited and narrowly circumscribed milieu) Derek, as well as many others like him, turned away from violent hustles to the relatively non-violent work of the marijuana trader. At the time I knew him, Derek was a small-time marijuana trader in East Dry River, competent and secure in his living. He had been doing this for several years. The fifties and early sixties were "bad john" years in Trinidad: violence was intrinsic to the street ambience and turf-based gangs ruled the streets. Police actions had something to do with bringing this phase to an end, but so too did the black nationalist cultural and political movement which generated new concerns and new priorities. Another cause was the increasing use of marijuana, called by many in East Port-of-Spain the "mellowing weed," which deflected easy propensities for violence to more contemplative modes of "laying back."

Beyond this, Derek's introduction to the Rastafarian credo made an enormous impression on him. In 1970 the Rastafarian movement was exclusively Jamaican. Few Trinidadians had much interest in or knowledge of the Rasta world view, but Derek became one of those few. Derek found the Rastafarian rejectionist attitude to Euro-Caribbean culture quite compatible with his own antagonisms, and he found its emphasis on African culture equally compelling. He liked the style, the music, the apparent quietude, pride and self-confidence of the Rastafarians. He became a Rasta proselytizer in East Dry River and began to gather a small following. He was one of those pivotal men found in Port-of-Spain's slums whose ego, insights and sense of where the action was—ideologically and spiritually as well as recreationally— were so compelling that others gravitated toward him and took stylistic cues from him.

The tensions inspired by the political disturbances of 1970–71 and by a series of convoluted legal and other practical problems Derek found himself facing, together with a sense of adventurousness, led him to decide to leave Trinidad. He moved to Montreal with Carl in the summer of 1971 and still resides there.

CLAUDE RUPPERT ("SNAKE")

Claude, or Claudie as he was usually called when not addressed or referred to by his monicker, "Snake," was one of Derek's closest friends. They shared a tiny one-room stucco house, and were partners in a fairly prosperous marijuana trading operation. Originally from Curepe, a town east of Port-of-Spain, he linked up with Derek soon after both arrived in the city.

Claudie had a big, bushy Afro hairstyle and dressed in jeans and a denim jacket most of the time, one of the "hipper" styles of dress that was especially favored by those who were politically active in their everyday affairs. While the nationalist intelligentsia favored dashikis and other African-derived accoutrements, their lumpen counterparts preferred denim. But Claudie had little interest in politics or in the sorts of cultural intrigues Derek found in Rastafarian ideas. Claudie was the complete hustler, smooth, practical, opportunistic and wary in all his dealings. Marijuana became pivotal in Claudie's life, nearly an obsession, and he generally only liked to involve himself in those scenes where getting high was paramount. But he was serene, relaxed, had a good sense of humor and a deeply sophisticated fondness for music, and he consequently served as something of a behavioral model for many youths in East Dry River. After Derek left for Canada, Claudie continued to run their marijuana operation; he still operates the business, much expanded, today.

ROBERT WINSTON ("RAT")

"Rat" (no one would consider calling him anything else) was a reknowned Port-of-Spain "street prince" and hustler. His reputation was city-wide; poor blacks loved him with the affection they reserve for a "character" who is bold and brazen but always true to his roots; the bourgeoisie thought of him as the epitome of the criminal element they were certain had overrun East Port-of-Spain. His name was often connected in the newspapers with some indictment or other, or with his status as an informal representative of the lumpen youth of East Port-of-Spain. Every policeman in the city knew about him. Many distorted stories were spun about his exploits, some portraying him as a saintly Robin Hood sort, others as a treacherous, monstrous ogre. During the 1971 disturbances it was rumored (and Rat admitted as much) that various downtown Syrian merchants paid him off to see what he could do to prevent the epidemic of fires that was sweeping the central business district from reaching their particular shops. They felt it was best to remain in Rat's good graces whether or not he himself had anything to do with the fires (he didn't), feeling that if anyone could direct and influence the course of events in East Port-of-Spain, he could. Just before the elections there was a front page article in the *Trinidad Guardian,* including several photographs, claiming that Rat was supporting Eric Williams and the PNM. The photos showed him together with several friends painting pro-PNM slogans on East Dry River walls and fences. This caused quite a furor, indicating Rat's position as cultural broker between the youth of East Port-of-Spain and the establishment. Many criticized and repudiated Rat's actions; his public show of support for the PNM was viewed as traitorous by those who assumed that Rat, if anyone, was "one of the people" and confidently expected to stand with them through the anti-PNM disturbances. While the political radicals felt betrayed, the PNM was just delighted. Rat's own version of what happened was much more straightforward and more in keeping with his character. He claimed that he had a serious court case pending and hoped that the facade of his public support for the PNM would benefit him. Of course he was right. This was a typical Rat mode of action. Above all the manipulator, unmatched in his street savvy and self-protective instincts, he always managed to remain on top of things, his reputation, at least while I was in Trinidad, never wavering among the lesser hustlers of the city.

Rat possessed a charismatic and highly admired personal style. He was tall and very uncomely and spoke with a deep, nervous stutter that made his speech difficult to understand. All this only made him more alluring, and figured as ingredients in his highly recognizable public image. He was the craftiest of hustlers, managing his presentations with consummate skill, cagy when he needed to be, bursting with seeming sincerity when that seemed appropriate. He maintained solid control over his social orbits through the force of his personality and his actions, and through thorough knowledge of his world. He made it his business to know as much as he could about what was happening, and he had excellent contacts in various circles—in the hustling world, among steelbandsmen and other musicians, among political radicals and, perhaps most importantly, within the police. He clearly knew the meaning and value of maintaining effective networks of information. Rat became a model of style and success for many young men in the area, and was immensely popular with friends and contemporaries such as Derek and Claudie.

Rat was in fact a small-time hustler. He peddled marijuana now and then, and gambled skillfully and cautiously but he had no aspirations to make much money. He lived humbly, not caring much for material accoutrements, but cherishing social recognition. Others were constantly doing him favors and he was well taken care of.

RICHARD GRANGER ("DUM-DUM")

Dum-Dum was one of Derek's very good friends from San Fernando and had followed him to the city. Dum-Dum, unlike most of the men in Carl's and Derek's circles, was a "bad john"—a tough, flamboyant, violent, bullyish sort of a man, more attracted to violent crime than to non-violent hustles. He was tolerated by many because of his close attachment to Derek, but others were wary of his unpredictable temper and recklessness. He was at the opposite end of the spectrum from the cool, patient style which was gaining favor now that the heyday of the bad john days was over. Dum-Dum was a big, powerful man, with a husky, threatening voice and a moody, excitable, aggressive disposition. Almost all of his visible teeth were capped in gold, which he thought to be quite charming, although by 1970 the gold capping of teeth was no longer very much in style and was viewed as garish by the young. Dum-Dum acquired his monicker after seeing a gangster film in which dum-dum bullets figured centrally in the action. The idea of a dum-dum bullet, which has a particularly nasty and destructive effect on impact, appealed to him and he took on "Dum-Dum" as a nickname. He was a successful hustler and many of his hustles involved violent crime. He had been a burglar and a stick-up man for years, but when I knew him he was trying to establish himself as a pimp. Prostitution does not ordinarily involve pimping in Port-of-Spain, but Dum-Dum became attracted to the pimp role and lifestyle while he lived in Canada and, upon returning to Trinidad, established himself as a pimp with some success. Some men admired him for his successful use of women as a source of exploitable income, but many more despised him for precisely this reason.

Dum-Dum lived in East Dry River for years, but soon after he began his pimping operation he bought a large house in the Carenage region at the western tip of the island. There he lived with several of his whores. Each night he brought these women to several clubs in town where they hustled for the night. Dum-Dum also maintained a pimping relationship with a few women that did not live with him but over whom he nevertheless exercised some control. From all this Dum-Dum had a large and easy source of income which allowed him to buy a house and drive an expensive British car. Dum-Dum ingratiated himself with rural women who drifted into Port-of-Spain; many of these were young East Indian women who left their villages as a result of some transgression or disagreement followed by ostracism (typically becoming pregnant by a non-Indian male) and these women, vulnerable and detached from their roots, were subject to Dum-Dum's charms and occasional coercions.

Dum-Dum was only at the fringes of the crowd that centered around Carl and Derek and Claudie. His unstable, rude, outdated bad john style was in marked contrast to their cultivated cool, and Carl, in particular, felt uneasy about Dum-Dum. It was Dum-Dum who smashed Carl's company car and Dum-Dum's carelessness caused Carl and Derek the trouble which led to their eventual departure for Canada. But Dum-Dum hosted Carl and Derek during their last two months in Trinidad when they were both rather down-and-out. Whatever his other faults, he was certainly generous to his friends. When Carl and Derek flew to Canada, Dum-Dum joined them, intending to stay for a short vacation, but he was rejected by immigration authorities upon his arrival in Montreal and was forced to return to Trinidad. Dum-Dum claimed that he wanted to "line up some white chicks" in Canada whom he could bring back to Trinidad with him, and hopefully send out hustling. He was bedazzled by the thought of pimping for white women and seeing them under his sway. Dum-Dum's fantasies were never corrected or illuminated by any interest or exposure to the broader ideological themes so prominent in Trinidad during this time. Others were beginning to link their sentiments to a wider informative context—they were becoming at least partly ideologized, their experiences contextualized in a framework of new meanings. Dum-Dum lacked this capacity utterly. Entirely self-centered, impulsive, unable to view things beyond the very narrow range of his own interests, Dum-Dum remained unaffected at a time when most others found the drifts of change unavoidable.

Following are some briefer vignettes of others who were parts of Carl's and Derek's "crew."[6]

"Catman" was associated with Carl and Derek since their earliest days in Port-of-Spain. He was a native of the city and had a very savvy knowledge of its social contours; it was he who first took Carl and Derek around to the downtown and eastern sections with which they would become so well acquainted over the years. Catman lived in a small house in a yard in downtown Port-of-Spain and from that yard operated one of the city's most active marijuana dispensing "ghettos."[7] Derek had frequent business dealings with Catman, whose knowledge of marijuana availability and awareness of other relevant contingencies related to the trade was usually accurate and up-to-date. Catman was always ready to articulate for others the benefits of the marijuana high, discussing its virtues in much appreciated, extended monologues. Others appreciated his eloquence and Catman himself dearly admired the Rastas who had made marijuana (for them a sacred "herb") central to their spiritual beliefs. Catman was indignant at what he felt were the hypocracies inherent in the way marijuana was condemned by the wider society, particularly its mainstream "enforcers." Catman saw as indicative of the general corruption of his society that someone like himself could wind up in serious legal trouble for selling or smoking a marijuana cigarette, while fatcat entrepreneurs who were among the cream of Trinidadian society could lavish in the wealth and respectability of their rum profits. Catman felt that rum was a sideline of the great Caribbean cancer—sugar—and that its dulling effects were perfectly meshed with the desire of those in power to have an unfocused, unideological, alcohol-dazed proletariat at their disposal. Marijuana, whose high, in his view, provided clarity and insight, was regarded as a threat. Attitudes toward marijuana, in general, were pivotal features in the construction of a worldview on the part of men like Catman, who saw the severely critical and punitive attitude toward marijuana and its users on the part of the power elite as another device to distort reality and to make life unnecessarily difficult for the man on the street.

"Slats" operated a ghetto in Woodbrook similar to Catman's and was also close to Carl and Derek. Small-scale marijuana peddlers such as Derek, Claudie, Catman and Slats generally felt a camaraderie of "deviants" who were all in the same boat, rather than the tensions and animosities of competition. For the most part, their outlets were located in different parts of the city and they tended to have mutually exclusive clienteles. Slats was an easygoing man and his devotion to music and gambling made him always ready to head out for a night of liming. He was mellow, comfortable and adaptable, very different than someone like Dum-Dum who was domineering, manipulative and who often engineered the direction of a lime so he could use it as a means to check up on his whores and take care of his other business. Slats lived a few blocks from his ghetto in a small room with a very pleasant, relaxed ambience about it; this, together with Slats' knack for nearly always having a number of very attractive women around him, made it a popular stopping-off spot for Carl and Derek and many of their crew.

"Mystic Man" had known Carl since he first arrived in Port-of-Spain and soon after became very close to Derek as well. Mystic Man was at thirty-eight the oldest, the most ideological and reflective, and in general the most unusual member of the crew. He developed a code of living which combined a sense of being African (albeit displaced); a committed belief in the powers of marijuana to clarify thought and feeling and to sharpen perception; a mystical and anticlerical religious approach; and a nearly unnerving quietude, gentleness and sense of balance. He was, as we say, remarkably "together." He wore a long beard and sometimes had his hair braided Rasta style. He could easily rise from his normal serenity to a stirring, prophetic excitability. He was a superb illustrator and his drawings of Rastafarians, assorted stylized African tribesmen, and of Malcolm X were displayed on the walls of Derek and Claudie's house. Apart from all this Mystic Man (his other name was Trevor) held a rather good job as a machinist. His participation in the crew's usual limes around town was limited. Mystic Man was more of a loner, content in his solitude and requiring much less socially-based action to fill his time than most other men. He was much more contemplative than most of his friends, who sometimes saw him as being nearly saintly. They respected him for this and acknowledged his limited willingness to socialize.

"Moose" was also older than most of the men in the crew and his participation in the crew's social world was limited as well, partly because he resided in Arima (a town twenty miles east of Port-of-Spain) and had his own crew in that town. But he came into the city at least once a week, and when he did he regularly limed with Carl, Derek and their friends. Moose ran a gambling club in partnership with a friend (what is called in Trinidad a "recreation club" requiring membership and where gambling can therefore be conducted legally). Carl and others in the crew regularly traveled to Arima to play cards at Moose's club. Moose's nickname reflects his strength and size. He was very cool and usually shrugged off taunts and threats that other men would view as signals to a fight, but he was a dangerous man when provoked beyond the limits of his normally unperturbable patience. His friends still talked about the particular incident that brought him his nickname. He was gambling at a club in Arima when a well-known and little-liked bad john walked into the club, revolver in hand, to stick up the players and walk off with the stakes. Moose grabbed for a cutlass (machete) beneath his chair and sliced off the man's arm, revolver and all. When I knew him, Moose was becoming more interested and involved with politics. He went through a reflective phase during which he began to criticize his previous cynicism and lack of interest in politics; he began to articulate increasingly committed views regarding the Trinidadian situation. Such changes were common during 1970-71, when the heat of events called forth responses from many of those who, with a skeptical and fatalistic shrug, had previously turned away from political and social involvement.

I began with Carl and suggested that he wavered between two social orbits: the street world of East Port-of-Spain and a more conventional world of bourgeois aspiration. Above I have tried to provide little vignettes of some of the men with whom Carl found himself linked in his street meanderings. Below I want to continue with some brief accounts of others in Carl's crew, men who, like him, were turning toward the bourgeois world and thus found themselves caught between two different modes of commitment.

ANDREW SULLIVAN ("REDS")

Apart from Derek, Reds was Carl's closest friend, and in many ways Reds's lifestyle was more in tune with Carl's than was Derek's, with its thorough commitment to the Trinidadian counterculture. The key problem in their relationship was that Reds simply could not control his feverish gambling; he was thoroughly hooked and during my stay began to slide deeper and deeper into the inextricable traps of gambling, becoming nearly a monomaniac in the process and losing touch with his friends and family. Carl remained loyal as Reds became more difficult, but Reds's need to gamble and his consequent lack of reliability, put a strain on their relationship.

Reds had gotten his monicker because of the complexion of his skin. In Trinidad men with such complexions are commonly referred to as "red-skinned" and are nicknamed "Reds." These are usually lower-class men with one dark (almost always the mother) and one light-skinned parent (as opposed to "colored" middle-class men who look very much the same, but are likely to have a different sort of genealogy—two colored parents—and are never referred to as red-skinned or addressed as "Reds"). Reds's mother was a black woman and his father was Portuguese. He was altogether reticent about his father (and his family background and past in general), and from what I could gather Reds was the outcome of a casual liaison between his mother and a white man. His two brothers, by a different father, were very dark. As a child Reds grew up in Woodbrook, living in one of the lower-class pockets in that generally middle-class area.

Reds, at first encounter, seemed rather conventional and middle-class—certainly not a ghetto type of man. He had a good, white-collar job and usually wore a white shirt and tie during the day. He had short hair and wore clear, plastic-framed glasses (as opposed to metal-rimmed glasses favored by young and stylish Trinidadian men). His wardrobe and other personal accoutrements suggested that he was quite different from all the other men I have so far described. But in fact Reds was not as square as he appeared. His street roots and his ease in dealing with many levels of Trinidadian society combined into a sophistication that made Reds at home in a wide variety of settings. And Reds's primary source in developing an ease and appeal in this multiplex world of social interactions was his striking facility for fluid talk. Reds could be spellbinding, and he always was, at the very least, comfortable with and in control of words. Such skill is very much appreciated in black Trinidad, where a premium is placed on lively and lilting conversation. Men sought Reds's company because they found him so compelling with his commentaries and his playful repartees. He invariably charmed and delighted those meeting him for the first time. Although he grew up in a largely middle-class neighborhood, attended a prestigious secondary school, and held a white-collar job as an assistant department manager for a major Trinidadian commercial concern, his personal style, and especially his verbal style, was quintessentially that of the ghetto. Reds grew up as a poor youth in a slum pocket of a generally inhospitable middle-class neighborhood. And though he was socially mobile and achieved some degree of conventional material success, he made a point not to "go bourgeois," as he put it.

Reds's ideas, sentiments and associations reflected his commitment to "roots," and a concommitant rejection of the proprieties and rewards of bourgeois respectability. He had the education and the resources to go the bourgeois route, as many in his circumstances have chosen to do. But he chose not to.

Reds's personal style, apart from his conversational gifts and the intelligence upon which these depended, included a skillfully manipulative demeanor in those situations where he was seeking something. This ability to maximize one's advantages is important in Trinidad, stemming from the slave system under which blacks relied on personal skills to turn their meager resources into the materials of survival and success. Such behavior was particularly noticeable in Reds's many encounters with women. Reds was married and had two children. He and his family lived in an apartment in Newtown but, with an increasingly unhappy marriage, he spent as little time at home as possible, though he always returned there to sleep after his nightly rounds of liming. He resented his marriage, was distant and cool toward his wife though warm and engaging with his children, and felt that his marriage restricted his behavior, especially in contrast to that of his unmarried friends. I often saw Reds become very sensitive when teased about the possibility that he might "not feel like going out" because so doing would bring about a scene with his wife. Nevertheless, Reds remained far more detached from his household and its commitments than did most married men. It was his wife's middle-class background and her family's insistence which propelled him to marriage. He spoke favorably of the more usual, and looser, common-law connections characteristic of poor Afro-Americans, an option he felt he was pressured out of by his wife and her family.

Reds was a well-known athlete, having excelled in cricket, swimming, soccer and other sports. His photograph and accomplishments have been featured in the sports pages of Trinidadian newspapers since he was a young teenager. He has been a star on many winning teams and represented Trinidad in regional competitions. His reputation as a top Trinidadian sportsman enhanced his prestige and popularity among all his social circles, and Reds made the most of this, playing up his reputation whenever this seemed advantageous, or when he was out creating impressions, as he so often was.

Reds illustrates several dimensions of what it is like to experience Trinidadian society while socially active and mobile. His social world was rich and diverse, and he felt comfortable among very different sorts of people in different settings. His lower-class background, embedded in bourgeois surroundings which he scanned and assessed as a child; his educational and vocational successes; his marriage to a comfortably middle-class woman; his involvement in sports and gambling; his pivotal role in labor union affairs; his reputation as a well-known and "likable sort of a guy," all propelled him into a fluid world of social experience encompassing many sectors and domains of Trinidadian society. Experience, style and accomplishment gave Reds access to diverse scenes and people, to a more sophisticated life. But through all this he developed specific priorities and commitments, which brought him to a recognition that the world of the streets and of the poor was *his* world. Carl, coming from a different but also very mixed encounter with all sorts of social scenes and experiences had come to a similar conclusion. It was partly this that brought Carl and Reds close to each other: they both had achieved some degree of ordinary material and vocational success; they could have opted for exclusively bourgeois styles and rewards; but instead they found Derek's East Port-of-Spain social world more alluring and more real.

Involvement in the social life of gambling clubs worked to unify lower- and middle-class social circles in Port-of-Spain. This was a world of men more than of classes. Both Carl and Reds could easily establish rapport with the very different sorts of men one might find around a gambling table—a street hustler, a Chinese merchant, a civil servant, a French Creole entrepreneur. But Carl could handle his involvements while Reds could not. Men greeted Reds—the athlete, the socializer, the storyteller—with an unusual show of welcome when he entered a gambling house. He glowed in all this adulation, but it also ultimately did him in.

RUPERT JOHN ("SMALLS")

Rupert was an active man, small of stature, befitting his years as a professional jockey. He had raced horses in Trinidad, Barbados and South America but never turned into the consummate pro his brother, a well-known and very successful jockey in North America, became. Smalls had worked as a part-time trainer at the Savannah racetrack after his stint as a jockey and also been a free-lance dealer in a number of the city's gambling clubs. Smalls, like Carl and Reds, was a chronic gambler but he was very good at it, able to profit from gambling by running games and working as a dealer rather than becoming a victim to the vagaries of gambling itself. For the last six months of my stay, Smalls ran a game for a major club owner at his downtown club. This, and not his training and racetrack work, was the major source of his income. Smalls was an exceedingly personable and unwaveringly cool and steady sort of a man, and others admired him for his disposition. His central position in Port-of-Spain's gambling and horse racing worlds elevated his popularity, and sometimes he and Reds would lime together, moving smoothly across various social scenes as well-known "celebrities." Smalls' participation in East Port-of-Spain scenes, in Derek's world, was only marginal but he felt comfortable and at home in these sorts of scenes and was always welcomed.

Smalls lived in downtown Port-of-Spain in a peculiar sort of building. It was a large, rambling apartment building, possibly the oldest still standing in the city. Most of the tenants were very poor and the building housed many small-time downtown hustlers of various sorts. Smalls lived in a large apartment with his common-law wife, his mother, and his six children. More than the other men in the crew, Smalls tended to be family-oriented. He had little rapport with his wife and was busily involved with one or more women outside of his marriage, but he adored his children and his mother and was hooked on television, so he tended to spend a considerable amount of time at home.

JOHN RAMSINGH

John's father was Indian, his mother Portuguese. He was the only member of Carl's crew who was not at least partly of African ancestry. John's attitudes reflected the difficulties he faced accepting a mixed genealogical background in a polyethnic society. Though he was half East Indian and bore an Indian surname, he often took a viciously anti-Indian stance in discourse; sneered at what he considered to be the style of Indian character and culture; rarely alluded to his Indian ancestry and when so doing passed it off whimsically as mere "accident." John was a well-educated man and could have been professionaly secure and successful. After finishing secondary school in Trinidad, he went to Canada for three years to receive additional training as a computer systems analyst. When he returned to Trinidad he obtained a job as a systems analyst for a government agency. He earned a very good income and lived in a very nice house in one of the affluent suburbs. When I knew him he had been married four years and had three children, but during my stay he and his wife became estranged and he moved out of his home and rented a room in Belmont. John had known Carl and Reds quite well in earlier years, but as he became more of a professional and more committed to family security and suburban status, he drifted away from them. But when he moved back into the city, he again began to associate with Carl and his crew and participated in the usual limes. Angered, depressed, confused by the disintegration of his family and marriage, John quit his job and completely turned away from his previous commitments to respectability and status. He began to hustle with a relish, claiming once again to feel free from the constraining tedium of bureaucratic employment; he was enjoying street life with the boys immensely.

John grew up feeling ethnically ambiguous. He claimed that Indian and white styles began to repulse him as he was growing up, and he turned away from what he saw to be the pretension and rigidity underlying these cultural outlooks. He said that "pure" Indians greeted his part-Indian status with contempt and ridicule. He despised his father and his father's family; he was a rebel in an Indian socialization context where rebellion is not usually tolerated. He took his punishments and refined his hatreds. At the same time John turned to education and always did very well as a schoolboy. At school and on the streets he felt more rapport with Afro-American boys than with Indians and Europeans. He found what he viewed to be the warmth and unpretentiousness of blacks highly appealing, and progressively drifted toward an orbit of associations which brought him ever more intimately into an Afro-American world. In the process he met Carl, Reds and Derek and became part of their circle. In short, he rejected the culture and circumstances of his family and upbringing, selecting other options from the arena of Port-of-Spain's cultural possibilities. He married a black woman and raised a family, he took education and professionalism seriously, but he never abandoned early resentments and appeals.

John was quite fond of marijuana smoking and this too served to bring him closer to blacks. After he moved to Belmont a series of circumstances made him pivotal in the East Dry River circles of men such as Derek, Claudie and Rat. John had befriended two small-time Venezuelan hoodlums who were staying in his rooming house. These men were purportedly in Port-of-Spain to learn English (many Venezuelans come to neighboring Trinidad to study English), but as it turned out they were wanted on assorted felony charges in Caracas (they robbed a bank and machine-gunned a guard and eventually were arrested on a charge of robbing a grocer in Port-of-Spain and extradited to Venezuela). These two men supported themselves in Trinidad by importing large amounts of marijuana to Trinidad from Venezuela. The marijuana was of a particularly high grade, much better than that grown in Trinidad. Very quickly the city's marijuana traders became aware of its availability and scurried to obtain as much of this highly marketable commodity as possible. John became the liaison between the Venezuelans and a number of Port-of-Spain traders. The Venezuelans spoke no English and John spoke fluent Spanish. His ties to Carl in particular, and through him to Derek, Claudie and Slats made him an especially important link and his company and friendship were valued by men in the crew. Through this initial role as a liaison, John was drawn closer to East Port-of-Spain's hustling world and became a regular participant in its scenes.

In some ways John was thrilled with his new lifestyle, but he was edgy as well. Family, education, professional competence vied with action, freedom, and the liveliness of the streets. John went through a phase where he totally abandoned his mainstream commitments and eagerly entered the street world, but other pressures and ambivalences endured, and eventually John returned to his wife and took his family to Canada, hoping that he could simplify his life there. He found work as a systems analyst with an electronics firm and lives now in Toronto.

Providing biographical and stylistic vignettes such as those above may seem an unusual mode of presenting ethnographically derived information. But I feel these scenes serve a purpose in conveying something of the concrete quality of flesh-and-blood lives. In attempting to illuminate patterns of social relations in a place such as Port-of-Spain, there is very little "system" or "structure" to speak of; this pattern of social relations cannot be presented as a crystalline matrix. We have here a loose and unstructured society, better described as a webbing or a mosaic than a rule-bound orderly package of emergent social possibilities. In some places—Bali comes to mind as an apt example—patterns of social and cultural relations seem to be describable in terms of a discrete architecture of arrangements. In others, and certainly in Port-of-Spain, such patterns have an amorphous and ambiguous quality, reflecting the multiple threads and influences found in urban Trinidad.

I would not claim that the men I have described above are members of a "group." I view a group as being determined by the regularity of encounters among members, a territorial base, commitments to common goals and plans, interdependent roles and the like. The links these men had to each other may better be described as a network, a social field within which connections unfold. Groups normally have some visible means of definition, as when gang members meet on a corner wearing the same jackets, or when Masons gather at a lodge, or when musicians play together; but networks are much more the personal constructs of people linked to others, or of ethnographers seeking to trace such linkages.

A network, like a kindred, must radiate from a center, from a single social unit (a person, a dyad, a "we"), extending itself outward to make connections. The men described above may be viewed as being linked to each other in a network which radiated from Carl or, perhaps even more correctly, from me. The ethnographer positions himself or comes to be positioned in a particular locus within the broader social field he is seeking to investigate. The view from this locus is a determinant of the shape of any network thereafter construed. In this sense, it is difficult to say whether one has "discovered" a network from the perspective of one's position (a common police view), or whether one's position is what gives that network its shape in the first place. Another vantage point would define a different network. The point, though, is not to justify the aptness of a particular network, but to put forward linked lives as illustrations of how biographies come to interconnect and influence each other in the continual flow of social activity.

I met Carl quite by accident. He immediately seemed to be the sort of man who could open doors, who could lead me on a wide-ranging circuitous tour through the Trinidadian social terrain whose scope and style I was seeking to understand. By meeting Carl and exploring the Port-of-Spain social world with him, I began to identify the linkages between Carl and those in his circles. Slowly I extended my relationships and knowledge to encompass those circles. A social network seen from Reds's point of view resembles and closely corresponds to Carl's, though of course there is no true overlap. Reds's network included many persons and classes of persons not included in Carl's network (those Reds worked with, for example). But Carl's links to Reds established a chain of relationships which increasingly involved them both. This is only a formal way of describing what we mean when we say "friendship." Surprisingly, friends rarely appear in ethnographies, though one hears enough about kinsmen, patrons and clients and other such more formal networks of relationships.

Carl's networks may be artificially divided into two broader components: those sets of men centrally involved in the East Port-of-Spain street culture (Derek and others), and those slightly older, more regularly employed, less "black," more "square" sets of men whose primary social turfs were gambling clubs and men's associations. These components, or circles, often merge as the capsule biographies suggest. One important pivot of differentiation is commitment to getting high on marijuana. For Derek and his crowd, marijuana and the values and behavior which surround its consumption are central to social experience. For others, marijuana consumption is more peripheral and not as critically related to a wider set of values. While there is certainly a good deal of overlap between values and styles—between commitment to ideals and the shaping and presentation of action and behavior—exceptions often emerge. John was well-educated and professionally inclined, but he had contempt for the status rivalries of the bourgeois world and much preferred the less competitive, more relaxed world of street scenes pivoting around getting high on marijuana and easy, fluid conversation. Dum-Dum, the supreme hustler, hungered for status and its material accoutrements, and he saw the confident, successful bourgeois swaggerer as an ideal of achievement.

Homes

For many poor, urban black men in Trinidad the idea of a home—a permanent place of residence to which much time and concern is committed—is not especially important. These men tend to view home practically and opportunistically, as a place at which to eat meals, to sleep and to have sexual relations. Often a man designates or thinks of several places as being home. He may be living in a rented room by himself though he does little more than sleep there, while taking his meals at his mother's, girl friend's, or aunt's house; or, very typically, eating out at an inexpensive snackette; and he may spend much time hanging out at the home of a more residentially stable friend. The locale of his action and activity is not the home, as it tends to be for middle-class men, but rather the streets and, in particular, a set of liming spots. Detachment and aloofness from a home base seems equally strange to middle-class people and to Trinidad's East Indians, who are extremely oriented to the household. But it should not be surprising. Raymond Smith (1956) has pointed out how for many poor, black men the household is more than anything a place in which inadequacies in fullfilling stereotypically defined male roles are stridently expressed, where weaknesses are most acutely exposed and least tolerated, and where the edifice a man builds up is constantly being eroded. The home often becomes a stage for scenarios of embarassment, harassment and humiliation. While in Trinidad the male's position in the household is not nearly as difficult as it has been described to be in other Afro-American societies, still the household tends to be a rather uncomfortable setting much of the time, a place where a man can expect to be reminded about his shortcomings.

Furthermore, a man's "real" home may seem a rather miserable place to occupy. It is likely to be overcrowded, marred by tensions, and demanding of his time. He prefers to avoid it. Much more interesting is the life of the streets, bars and clubs. Here a man enjoys a greater fluidity of movement; here he is subject to fewer demands and finds he has more choices; and here he encounters a repertory of routine and exceptional events and occasions which he is likely to find engaging.

Carl is typical in this regard. During most of my stay in Trinidad, Carl lived in a couple of shabby rooms in a dilapidated house in Belmont with a woman and her two children. The house was a rowdy, sleazy sort of place; it was overcrowded, and the presence of several particularly raucous prostitutes made it noisy and active during the late hours. Carl frequently complained, claiming that he could not take all the "shit talk" that went on in the place (everytime I went there someone seemed to be bawling, arguing, fighting). Carl wanted to stay far away from all the malicious gossiping and arguing among the tenants. Apart from the highly unpleasant ambience of the building, Carl was getting on poorly with his lover. Increasingly he wished to get away from the entire scene and away from Anne, who he felt was putting pressure on him to make some sort of firm commitment to her just as he was losing interest. Eventually they had a falling out and she and her children moved out and went to live with relatives elsewhere in Trinidad. Carl also left the house (he had originally moved in as a convenience, to join Anne who already resided there). He moved to St. James, taking a small room in a large, new, middle-class home of an East Indian family who took in boarders. Carl found his new landlord and his family quite agreeable and they in turn took to him. Carl tended to get along much better with East Indians than did most black men, having been brought up among them in San Fernando. But he viewed his new room as little more than a place in which to sleep, rest, wash and store his things. He rarely ate there, and it was difficult for him to smoke marijuana or entertain women. His landlord was nice enough, but closely scrutinized his tenant's movements. In some ways Carl's real home was his company car. When Carl got behind the wheel of his Renault he felt at home, free, fluid, his own man—living out an image of the function and ambience of the automobile which is certainly familiar to North Americans. Carl's lifestyle had developed over the years around the necessity for a car and the mobility it provided. And most of Carl's friends, who did not have cars of their own— who lived in a social environment where owning a car was exceptional—came to depend on Carl for transportation and mobility. The Renault became an occasional home for many men.

Reds's home in a quiet, serene neighborhood was comfortable enough, and he did appreciate occasional, but only occasional, peace and quiet. Reds, though, viewed his household commitments as constraints. He felt that his wife harangued him (she did, and certainly had justification, for he was a chronic liar and a rogue with women), and that his house was too far away from any decent action. When Carl, Reds and others began to stop by at my place regularly, they commented on how unusual it was for any one of them to spend much time in each others' homes. Even though Reds had known Carl for years, and had been one of his closest friends, he was only inside his house on two occasions, and those times to briefly pick up a few things. Although Carl called on Reds almost nightly to scoop him up for the evening limes, he had been *inside* his house only once. Normally he knocked on Reds's door and waited until Reds was ready to join him. This suited them both, for there was tension between Reds and his wife over Reds's various evasions and extra-marital adventures, and Carl represented the connection that made these adventures possible.

Such a pattern, based on an inclination to view one's home as necessary but peripheral, and to spend as little time as possible inside it, distinguished the social movements of most men. However, there were exceptions, and some men found their homes quite satisfying and had much more of a "home and hearth" attitude toward them. Some found themselves very close to their wives and lovers, particularly when sex was satisfying. Others preferred privacy within walls to the unpredictability of the streets. An appealing lover, a place where one would not be hassled, the ownership of a stereo— all these were compelling factors for those men who simply enjoyed staying home. Even more important was the availability of a suitable ambience in which to relax and to smoke marijuana with friends, although this was sometimes difficult to achieve because of disapproving wives or nosy neighbors.

Whereas Reds and Carl were always eager to "go out," men such as Derek and Catman, though certainly never ones to turn down the opportunity to seek some satisfying action, appreciated their homes as places where they could entertain in privacy and relax with friends and lovers. Since an enhanced interest in marijuana smoking necessitated a change from traditional forms of outdoor or public liming (hanging out on corners, going to public parties and to the movies) to a greater focus on private, concealed environments shared by a small number of intimate friends, an appealing home became a desired convenience. In 1968, when Derek and Claudie were becoming more involved in marijuana smoking and trading, they began to pull away from much of their previously public lives and decided to purchase a small house where they could live together, socialize with their friends in a private setting, and set up a base of operations for marijuana distribution. For $300 they bought a tiny house in East Dry River, on the edge of the downtown district (a requirement for them since proximity to downtown "action centers" was necessary in order to be on top of things in the development of a successful marijuana operation). One could only euphemistically refer to their home as a house. It was a detached structure consisting of nothing more than one very small room about ten feet long and varying in width from about four to seven feet. There was a sink inside and a toilet and improvised shower outside. But Derek and Claudie made maximum use of available space, installing bunk beds, a wall-to-wall carpet (they insisted that visitors remove their shoes upon entering), a big stereo phonograph console, a portable battery-powered record player, two radios, a television, a cassette tape recorder, a shelf of books, and such furniture as a dresser, a small table, one chair and assorted knick-knacks. The use of space produced a cozy intimacy rather than the overwhelming crowdedness and disorder one might expect. The room was carefully decorated with drawings of Rastafarians, National Geographic photographs of African tribesmen, and portraits of Malcolm X, Mahatma Ghandi, Frank Zappa and Ras Tafari himself—the Emperor Haile Selassie of Ethiopia. Derek and Claudie kept a big Doberman pinscher for protection and on a few occasions needed the dog for just this reason.

Claudie did not spend too much time at the house and preferred to lime with Rat at his place a few blocks away (wherever Rat was there were sure to be lots of people and lots of action, and this appealed to Claudie). But Derek spent much time at home, including most of the daylight hours. This was necessary since customers continually came by and Derek needed to be available much of the time to make sure things were in order, though Gelden and Panhead, his two young assistants and proteges were always around to take care of business when Derek went out. Derek was very attached to his little home; he liked the way he and Claudie had furnished it; he felt comfortable in its tranquility, having grown a little tired of the club and bar scene that many of his agemates, and especially slightly older men, found so engaging. At home Derek had his music, his marijuana, and his close friends; and Derek's social and personal life had recently put a premium on these three sources of satisfaction. It is men who have homes such as Derek's, and attitudes toward their homes such as his, who attract the "floaters"—men, who for one reason or another, see their homes more as prisons than as castles and consequently seek to escape them, finding surrogate homes in their cars, or in clubs, or if they are fortunate, in the homes of friends who have somehow transformed the idea of a ghetto home from a prison to a castle—something Derek had succeeded in doing particularly well. Derek put it this way:

> When I was younger I was wild. You couldn't keep me inside unless it was a card game in a club or in a room with a whore, or seeing a flick. People would come around asking, "Where's Derek?" And I would always be out cruising and looking for something to do, always out for kicks, hot-headed and getting into trouble. I'm finished with that now. I still like to go out on a cool lime with a cool head. But now with the weed I'm happy just staying home, spending time with some good partners, and listening to Isaac Hayes [an American "soul" singer whom Derek particularly liked].

The Streets

Nevertheless, most men have not, like Derek, been able to create satisfactory personal environments, and their lives continue to be based in the streets, in public terrains of action. The streets are their living room. Street life is not limited to the streets in the literal sense; a street focus includes events and scenes that take place in public niches such as bars, clubs, Calypso tents, movie theaters, and so forth. Street life is then to be contrasted with home life. Much of the day-to-day experience of young men is focused on street life. Such an attachment is not limited to only *young* men, but a lesser commitment to certain conventional domains of social life—such as family and church—and a greater desire for appealing, energizing modes of action make young men the prototypical exemplifiers of street styles. Wilson has argued, in citing another Caribbean case (1969), that young men eventually mellow and become more staid, and as they pass through their life cycle they settle down, abandon the reckless world of peers and pleasures, and take family and religious commitments more seriously. This may be true, but we will not really know until Derek and Carl and the others grow older.

The emphasis on street life, especially in the literal sense, distinguishes the style of commitment among lower-class men (and, much less so, women). The poor, with minimal resources and often uncomfortable residential conditions, are especially apt to make full use of the free or cheap resources of street life as readily available means of spending time in an interesting and engaging manner. In the anthropologist's search for cultural worlds of meaning, the humdrum time-killing activities that make up so much of a twenty-four-hour day are sometimes ignored in favor of more spectacular or symbol-laden plans and events. But the ethnographer cannot ignore anything that takes up the bulk of the day, regardless how mundane it appears, without painting a distorted picture of what life looks like for those who live it.

A Trinidadian woman's opportunities for seeking fulfilling modes of action are often hindered by male-imposed social conventions limiting her social fluidity and experimentation, and by her involvement in the maintenance of households and the organization of family life. Middle-class people often have more appealing home situations, and are, more significantly, *expected* to orient themselves around their homes, which tend to serve as badges of status and signs of stability. And members of the middle-class also have the resources to seek amusement in certain conventionalized ways that contrast sharply with street-based options. But poor men have often been limited to the diversions of the streets by necessity, and that necessity has evolved into a cultural choice. This ingredient of choice is crucial. Social analysts, looking sadly at what seems to them the disorganized ambience of street life often argue that poor men are "forced" or "driven" to the exigencies of street life since other possibilities are closed to them. As urban sociologists, influenced by the concerns of social reform, so often put it, poor men wind up on the streets because there are no mechanisms to keep them within the confines of more conventional (and, from a bourgeois point of view, more acceptable) social zones. There is certainly some truth here, but such a focus ignores *choice* as a factor in the selections men make regarding their social ambience. It is not that poor men find themselves on the streets because there is nothing else to do and nowhere else to go, and then attempt to make the best of their situations; rather, they choose the streets because action unfolds in the streets. For those freed from unquestioning obedience to cultural codes specifying exactly what their daily round of activities and commitments should be like, life often appears as a struggle against tedium. What others accept as "ought," these men largely reject, and with their rejection they seek alternative lifestyles of their own making. Knowing that opportunities present themselves to those who are attuned to the flow of events unfolding in the streets, men seek to take best advantage of the street's social resources. In Goffman's terms, these men are on the lookout for "where the action is."

Liming

I have referred to liming and taking a lime numerous times in the preceding pages. Liming may best be glossed as "just hanging around," but hanging around with eyes and ears keenly tuned to the flow of action and the recognition of advantage. The limer is attuned to making something eventful of street life. The highly visible groups of young men who gather on street corners and on stoops, or in front of snackettes and cinemas all over the city are tagged and tag themselves as limers. Ask a group of familiar young men what they are doing when encountered lounging idly on a street corner; they are apt to tell you they are just liming. The casual and seemingly idle stance of such postures confuses and antagonizes a hostile bourgeois public, and for the most part has failed to interest anthropologists who tend to be more interested in the peaks of social experience than the lulls. Middle-class attitudes favor the view that liming is delinquent activity—the wasting of time by men and boys who are doing nothing but should be doing something. Often there are "No Limers" or "No Liming" signs posted by snackettes or other shops whose owners feel that men are likely to seek out as particularly suitable liming spots. These zones where liming is concentrated are pivotal points in the "action topography" of the city. It is at such points, marked by their visual accessibility to indices of action (major street intersections, assorted social niches where people tend to congregate and through which crowds routinely pass), where limers tend to concentrate their scanning of scenes. Through such scanning, men learn, day by day, what sorts of intriguing events await their participation. Furthermore, men tend to secure a favorite liming spot, a location where those who seek them in the course of a day know they may be found, at least sporadically. Such a location may become, in a sense, a man's street address. In a social world where telephones count for little, and yet the ability to make quick contact with a variety of loosely-linked people is important, men need to know how to find significant others.

A man sensitized to action, then, seeks routinely to locate himself at street points where interesting encounters are likely to happen, and where news of promising scenes is likely to be in the air. Two key expressions in the Afro-American slang of Trinidad (and of United States black argot as well)—"what's happening" and "checking out the scene"—summarize such an orientation. These phrases convey, in acutely sociological and richly condensed terms, the readiness and anticipation with which people seek to transform the passing world into a world of encounters and events. In the streets scenes are public; they are not sheltered acts behind closed doors. The extent to which a man is tuned into the information circuits of the streets affects his potential involvement in interesting scenes. These men know they must develop techniques of embedding themselves in promising social terrains if they are to get close to potentially involving happenings. This process is like stalking about a hunting ground for its game potential; in this case the game is action. The search for action reflects a key disposition among black men in Trinidad, just as elsewhere the avoidance of action in favor of a secluded, predictable round of life is the aim of other dispositions.

Liming may also point to a mobile style in which men move from scene to scene in an attempt to discover what is happening where. The key expression here is to "take a lime." This involves a group of men deciding to spend part of a day or night in a focused search for appealing events. The search is very clearly for scenes, and this points to the episodic fashion in which Trinidadian men organize time and its punctuations. And, again, the aim is activity with a vector and with pulses and pauses, rather than a steady constancy (Bateson's notions of cultural "steady states" and their opposites come to mind). The strategy behind taking a lime seems to be more productive and more efficient as a means of discovering what is happening than is embedment at a single spot. This latter mode of liming, the "hanging around" variety, is more typical of younger men and adolescents who are making initial attempts to develop a workable sense of the action-topography for themselves by observing the passing of events from a relatively stable vantage point. That is why Gelden and Panhead, Derek's two assistants, were so keen on just liming at Derek's ghetto and helping him out, expecting no compensation beyond a few sticks of marijuana. They knew the spot was pivotal; by embedding themselves there they were in a position to learn about various contexts of opportunity. Older men, who already have this knowledge and a good knack for where to search out action, and who have some money and easier access to adult scenes, tend to alter the liming pattern, becoming more mobile and making an active attempt to seek action rather than waiting for news of action to come to them. Serious, mobile limers inevitably make their way to one or more of the city's numerous "ghettos" during their daily meanderings through the city's scenes.

The word *ghetto* has taken on a special meaning in Trinidad and is used to refer to certain sorts of liming spots where "cool heads," or those viewed as being especially in tune with street-specific and anti-mainstream styles, are apt to gather. The core activities here are marijuana use and distribution and the constellation of events revolving around music. These ghettos are usually key points in marijuana distribution circuits, as well as meeting spots for those committed to the especially active musical scene that serves as a broad esthetic backdrop for much of the action of the Port-of-Spain street world. While Trinidadian music is not a special concern in this book, I should emphasize that the island's musical ambience is unusually dynamic. It is difficult to convey this to those who have not been there, but all those who have are astonished by the quantity and diversity of music produced, and the importance that music has in everyday life. A similar ambience exists for all of the Caribbean region. Recently the stylistic development of popular music and a growing interest in marijuana have come to be linked. These linkages are strikingly evoked in the ambience of Port-of-Spain's many ghettos where "sounds" and "smoke" together have come to activate the texture of much liming activity.

The ghetto's function as a key point in a marijuana distribution network contributes special qualities to its tone as a hang-out locale. Limers are attracted to ghettos, and the pivotal men who control ghettos actively seek clients, but they are simultaneously worried about exposure and the dangers of involvement in illegal enterprises. Consequently, ghettos are located in relatively sheltered alleyways or in the small yards between and behind houses. But they cannot be too carefully insulated and obscured, since clients and other interested parties must have access if the ghetto is to function as the location of an enterprise. Music, by both its sound and the activity its rehearsal and performance generates, tends to diffuse the focus on marijuana sales at ghettos, and can serve as somewhat of a front, allowing partial concealment of more sensitive activities. Nevertheless, ghettos as locales of illegal activities are vulnerable to mainstream intrusion. Therefore only certain sorts of men— those with well-integrated action dispositions (see Goffman on what such dispositions involve, 1967:214)—choose regularly to pass time at such spots. The strong appeal of these ghettos as focal liming spots partly rests on the public knowledge that the key men in the city's street scenes—those around whom action pivots—typically make one of these ghettos their base of operations; and these men's assorted involvements and interests generate much of the action available for others' engagements.

As Horton has pointed out, many ghetto men operate within "street time" (1967:9), and the units of measure for this sort of time are not quite the same as units of mainstream time. Mainstream time is linked to the contingencies of employment and family life, and these may not be the most relevant of concerns for street-based men who are not primarily moved by demands stemming from job and family. Many poor, urban men realize that mainstream concepts of order, sequence and time stem from the needs of bourgeois modes of regulating activity and may not be particularly salient to their way of life. The rhythm of street life is not so much patterned by the expectations and responsibilities generated by mainstream social orbits as it is by the flow of concrete events, people and resources that convert tedium into interest and dead time into significance for limers. Time on the streets is highly episodic, and liming reflects this episodic quality.

A detailed description of liming tracks seems fitting here. The following two accounts are abbreviated excerpts from my field notes jotted down after rich, but fairly typical evenings of liming with members of the crews of men I have discussed in the previous pages:

> I ran into Kevin and Derek on Queen Street in front of the little snackette where they sometimes limed during the day. They were talking with some of the boys from East Dry River who had set up a stand here and were selling "Afro" leather goods. Derek told me the two of them had been killing some time here until they could link up with Carl when he was through working at the car lot. Derek said they were planning to drive to San Juan to play cards at a new club Fernandes had told them about. I said I'd join them and the three of us walked toward Woodbrook to meet up with Carl. We stopped to eat some Roti [a popular East Indian snack], and Derek said he wanted to detour over to Catman's ghetto on Tragerete street to see if he could find some weed. Derek had been out of stock all week, and was becoming edgy about not being able to turn on his regular customers; said that weed had been hard to come by for the past week since the big bust on Nelson Street cut supplies and made all the traders nervous. Catman was at his place, but he was of no help and said that he in fact was hoping to get something from Derek. Much small talk about the recent string of police busts, who was behind them and when things might cool down. Catman said he'd lime with us since things were dead at his ghetto, and he hoped he might run into some action in San Juan. We said we'd stop back for him with the car after we picked up Carl. We walked over to the square and limed there for a while until we saw Carl pull up in his Renault. We got in and Carl said he had promised to look up Reds at the Savannah after work. We drove there and found Reds talking to a few Indians. He joined us and told us the Indians had said there had been a stabbing at the San Juan club last night, and that it would be a good idea to stay away from there tonight

since the club was over in Maraj's territory, and they expected things
to get very hot over there with the Indians feuding and now the
stabbing. That was all we needed to know. Kevin was especially relieved
since he generally liked to stay away from Indian territory and had
been shaky about the San Juan trip to begin with. It was dark now
and we decided to head over to Catman's place to tell him the
San Juan trip was off, and see if he had come up with anything.
Things, it turned out, were active at his ghetto. Catman was sitting
in front of a big paper bag full of weed and dividing it up into
parcels. He told us that since we were last there a couple of hours
ago he ran into something, and Derek's eyes lit up. A couple of men
I had never seen before were picking up parcels. We spent the next
hour or so there passing around the "spliffs" Catman was busy
rolling, and listening to some Temptations tapes a friend of Catman's
had sent him from Brooklyn. Much talk about music, about how
appreciated these battery-run tape recorders were since they made
sounds portable, about the Meters coming from New Orleans to play
in town next week, about plans Derek and Catman were making to
drive to an Indian grower near Rio Claro to see if they could pick
up some bulk marijuana at a good price, about Kevin's troubles with
Jean and Carl's self-proclaimed successes with a woman he met at a
Maraval fête last week. And much talk about hashish. Many of the
traders were talking about it. Not many had seen it or used it, but
since word of a small shipment of exceptionally high quality hashish
from Venezuela had spread, all the traders seemed deeply intrigued
by this new version of a cannabis high and were scrambling to get
some. Derek said that Dum-Dum had some, and Catman convinced
Derek and Carl to go and try to find Dum-Dum and see if a link
could be made. Much driving around trying to find Dum-Dum at the
downtown and East Dry River ghettos. Finally we spotted him at
one of his liming spots on Basilon street but he told Catman and
Derek that he couldn't help them out, and asked us instead to give
him a ride to a party in Belmont. With Carl's Renault now packed,
we went there, and the party turned out to be more like a seminar
with a Rasta guy from Jamaica talking to a few people about the
Kingston scene. Derek was intrigued, and over Kevin's objections
[Kevin always feels uncomfortable around philosophical talk; it
grates at his residues of conventional Christian beliefs.] convinced
us to stay for a while. Derek has become more and more interested
in the Rastas and their scene, and is plaiting his hair now and putting
up Rasta drawings on his walls. A lot of Trinidad-Jamaica compari-
sons were tossed out for consideration over the next hour, and then
we left, after Carl made it clear that he still wanted to get over to a

club that night. We went over to one of the big Chinese tourist
clubs and walked in on a tired scene with a very limp band playing
music. Carl walked over to the back room and found out from
Wally, the Chinese owner, that a game had opened up. So we all
went back there and watched Carl play some poker and win a few
dollars. He was delighted and bought beers for us all. It was Thurs-
day and the consensus was not much else would be going on at this
late hour, so we got into the Renault and Carl dropped us all off
at our homes.

And on another night:

Carl stopped by at my place and we walked over to Belmont
together to one of the panyards. Being mid-January and Carnival
only a few weeks away, all the Calypso tents and steelyards were
especially active and during these last few weeks liming has tended
to focus on music. Derek was already listening to the carefully
orchestrated rehearsal, as were about thirty other onlookers. Hanging out at the panyards was especially satisfying at this time of the
year as musicians gear up for Carnival. Derek was involved in one of
his typical musical disputes, arguing with someone that the steelbands were looking for false respectability with their attempts to
master "light classical music." Derek was arguing that whenever the
middle-class wanted to cite the achievements of Trinidad's own steelband music they pointed to how the players had mastered Chopin
and Tchaikowsky and things like that. Derek claimed this was
typical; artistic "seriousness" and quality always seemed to depend
on how closely musicians conformed to European standards and
styles. The other man was unconvinced, and was off on an ethereal
apologia for the glories of European musical accomplishment, claiming that Derek should be proud that Trinidadian musicians could
achieve a mastery enabling them to play European music in a unique
way. Derek scoffed at this, feeling it was just one more example of
distorted, European-focused thinking. Carl laughed it off and asked
Derek if he wanted to go down to the tent and hear Kitchener and
his boys [Lord Kitchener is perhaps Trinidad's foremost Calypsonian;
a "tent" is an enclosure, usually a large yard with a raised roof otherwise used as a market area or something of that sort, which is transformed in the weeks before Carnival into a staging area for Calypso
reviews]. We went there and the tent was packed, everyone saying
this was going to be Kitchener's year [Calypsonians compete with
each other during the pre-Carnival period and these evenings in the
tent are both performances aimed to familiarize and draw audiences
to the songs of the season, while also serving as rehearsals to give

musicians a chance to polish up their material and gauge audience
response]. We listened to Kitchener and a few others and they were
good. The Calypsos have certainly been tending toward politics and
ideology this year. We ran into "Reacher," who was working for
Kitchener's tent, collecting tickets, helping out with equipment and
the like. Reacher had only one arm; he lost the other in his bad john
days with the cut of a cutlass, and since then has very much subdued
his ways. Derek was in a critical mood. Reacher, who often limed
with Derek at his place in East Dry River, asked Derek what he
thought of the scene that night. Derek complained that Calypso
was becoming stale, the same old postures and orchestrations. He
said Jamaican music was innovative, imaginative, and was going to
steal the thunder from Trinidadian music [from the perspective of
1979 it certainly looks as though Derek was right in his assessment
nine years ago]. He complained that Calypsonians had an aloof,
mocking attitude toward the critiques carried by their lyrics and that
in these times such an attitude was inappropriate. Reacher took us
to a back room and rolled up a spliff. He said he had to finish up
a few things and then would like to join us. The tent was about to
close. The four of us left and went to St. James to see "Rasta
Charlie," a Jamaican friend of Derek's. Charlie wasn't in, but we
stopped and talked with his sister Vivian. Carl and Reacher laid out
the charm, responding to Vivian's exceptional attractiveness, but she
handled them with a gracious sort of aloofness, they got the message
and settled down, realizing there were no opportunities here and no
need for male strutting, and began joking around with Vivian easily.
Charlie's place was plastered with illustrations of Rastafarians, lions,
Jamaica village scenes, and a shelf containing a number of books on
mysticism and biblical commentary. We left a message for Charlie
(he and Derek had some business to transact in regard to a small
shipment of marijuana Charlie had just received), and then Carl
made the mistake of asking Vivian, with a very self-confident and
seductive tone, if she would "like to spend some time with him"
later in the week. She lashed out at him with a tirade about his
presumption and general remarks about the exaggerated expectations men have about easy accessability to women, asking Carl
mockingly about "exactly what it was he had to offer," and then
answering for him by suggesting that it was likely nothing she needed
or wanted. A little humbled but basically unperturbed—Trinidadian
men are accustomed to such repartees—Carl withdrew and apolo-
gized with a little smile; Vivian accepted the apology and calmed
down, and with another round of goodbyes we left. We wound up
in a bar in East Dry River where we found Panhead and Gelden

playing tunes on the jukebox. The next hour or so were devoted
to playing songs by American artists with comments from all sides
about comparative genres, styles, quality of musicianship, and the
like. Rat walked in and told us he thought the police were going to
come down hard after some of Granger's boys [Granger, a militant
black nationalist, headed NJAC, a radical political organization]
following the fires last night on Henry Street. He told everyone to
stay cool since the police were in a busting mood. And then Rat
arranged with Derek and Carl to go see some Indians near Sangre
Grande about some weed. This purchasing trip was planned for the
weekend.

I included these excerpts here as hopefully evocative illustrations of the
sorts of scenes encountered and constructed by some Trinidadian men, and
as examples of how sequences of activity (or patterns of action) emerge
from the rather loose explorative stance toward social participation and
maneuver which links these men in activity, and generates a particular sort
of social ambience.

One feature distinctive of limes and liming is its ad hoc character. A lime
is generally a loose, vaguely planned—though carefully assessed—string of
engagements. It is just the sort of style of social action one would expect to
see unfolding in an urban context which is polyethnic, expanding, uncon-
solidated, and where movement into the city, and within it, is fluid and
active. Antrhopological exploration of such styles has largely been neglected
in Caribbean ethnography. In focusing on household composition, family
networks and formal groups, ethnographers in the region have for the most
part ignored the crucial, interstitial role of street life as a sociocultural arena.
For gauging how time is spent, and thereby devising at least one way of
determining social commitments, an emphasis on how street scenes unfold
is important for any understanding of what urban proletarian men in a
locale such as Port-of-Spain are up to. It is largely on the streets, rather than
inside homes, that much of the socially significant action that occupies men's
time emerges. As Suttles noted in his study of Chicago's "Addams" area,
exposure to street scenes bridges the privacy of more secluded family-bound
domains (Suttles 1968:73). Here people open themselves up for inspection
in public displays of activity-seeking, and here men learn, through their interpretive assessment of occasions and events, what the composition of social
life is like in an urban setting, and how such a setting may be approached as a
resource. It is through this assessment of particular events and encounters,
what Suttles calls "private disclosures," that men develop normative expectations and standards revealing what life's possibilities really add up to; and this
version is apt to contradict more formal, mainstream standards of public
morality encountered in more conventionally structured social domains. Such

normative and stylistic contradictions among collections of cultural guide-
lines available for scanning and adoption are a key feature of urban life in
bourgeois societies.

These accounts of liming may appear to depict humdrum activities, merely
ways to pass the time of day or night, and unworthy of ethnographic recognition. But such activities are far from trivial. First of all, liming patterns, as
the ethnographer interprets them, reveal specific stylistic orientations reflecting commitments and choices regarding what is appealing and what is not.
That is, in liming we see where much of meaning, in the Weberian sense, is
grounded for men such as these. We ignore an important dimension of social
style if we regard street life embedments as merely ways of making do in
rough times, rather than as outcomes of choices to design sociability in
particular ways.

Furthermore, many of the key concerns in liming, as should be clear
from the excerpts, involve judging available social and economic opportunities, deviant though these may be from a mainstream perspective. In assessing
what's happening and in checking out various scenes, men also aim to take
care of business; they determine what sorts of resources are available and
what sorts of situations are advantageous. For them, such determination is
continuously problematic, but also engaging. Street-based men may not be
securely lodged in predictable and repetitive life-patterns involving family,
employment and conventional role and status constellations, but the reward
of what some may choose to see as an alienation from communal order and
structure is the capacity to enjoy a measure of flexibility which many persons, caught up in bourgeois-generated expectations, do not have available
to them.

Limers tend to see the social world as a maze of possibilities to be discovered. Not caught in exact routines, and continually examining the texture
of the social terrains they occupy in order to assess the potential for themselves, they tend to be keen observers of social scenes. The standard proletarian greeting in the streets of Port-of-Spain, "Yo! Wha' appenin," tends to
be much more than an empty formality. It is a call for information, a signal
to expand perspectives cooperatively and to match assessments of commonly
encountered situations, and thereby to carve out of the residues and resources
deposited through several hundred years of oppression a mode of life which
is not simply a set of distorted adaptations sustained by a false conciousness—
an unworkable mimicry of a mainstream culture, a veneer without sub-
stance—but a life which affords some measure of choice and flexibility in
the arrangement of time and activity. Black and poor, the odds are heavily
stacked against these men in any attempts they make to achieve conventional
success. Knowing this, they are concerned to redefine continually what
success and satisfaction may and may not mean, and with these assessments
available as guiding standards, to engage the social world in a critical manner.

Ghetto "Types"

What unifies those who are committed to ghetto life is an alienation from rewards of a mainstream life, and a consequent turning to other sources of satisfaction, which revolve around a constellation of action and sociability marked by "hipness" (Other rejections of mainstream concerns involve immersions in worlds of piety and religious devotion.). Though ghetto men run a range of styles and stances, it may be useful to isolate, by abstraction, three ideal "types" of men, each distinguished by a particular configuration of style.

The "saga boy" is a young, well-dressed sport, a ghetto dandy. He has flair and tends toward exhibitionism; he's up-to-date in regard to styles and likes to surround himself with women. He is usually dressed to kill and keenly aware of his physical appearance. He loves the limelight and relishes attention, particularly that of women. He's seductive, extroverted, comfortable with himself (at least so appearances suggest), a master of impression management. His style is similar to the "pimp" style as it is sometimes referred to in black, North American ghettos, though with many fewer accoutrements— no Cadillac Eldorados or diamond pinky rings. The saga boy projects a highly stylish external image, and develops competence in controlling "face" in such a way as to be able to control and manipulate others. Though saga boys are admired to some extent by ghetto audiences and onlookers, particularly when they manage to carry off the image with impeccable precision, they also face a good deal of contempt for their dandyness, their obviousness, their unconcealed concern for how they appear to others. These features point to flaws in integrity and self-confidence, weaknesses obscured and at the same time evoked by displays of garish theatricality.

The "bad john," a popular type a few years ago but now rapidly going out of style and moving to the periphery of acceptability, is the Trinidadian tough guy. During the days of turf-based street gangs, he was predominant; with a shift in the ambience to less violence, his limelight is rapidly fading. Bad johns are men who seek what they want, attempt to get it through force, and aim to create impressions of their toughness. Such men have ambiguous reputations in Port-of-Spain's ghettos. While the bad john's toughness and arrogance point to qualities occasionally admired (and often necessary) in the city's streets, such men exaggerate these qualities to the point of disturbing social scenes with the aggressive largeness of their presence. The bad john is brutal rather than manipulative; he is "hot" rather than "cool." Commonly, saga boy and bad john styles are combined into an amalgam yielding someone very much like Dum-Dum: a man who is tough, crude, flashy, excessively demonstrative, sometimes violent and always potentially dangerous, obsessively focused on the presentation of his maleness. He exhibits an exaggerated concern with appearances and is unable or unwilling to conceal this overblown concern. His style tumbles in upon itself, eroded and weakened by the obviousness of its display.

The "hustler" is a different sort of character. His ideal qualities are manipulativeness, cleverness, and "cool." His manipulativeness is not primarily concerned with coercing or cajoling others to do what he pleases, but to be able to position himself so as to best reach out for advantage. Unlike the bad john, the hustler is not particularly concerned with displaying his toughness and prefers to avoid violence if possible; unlike the saga boy he would rather blend unobtrusively into the background than to strut like a peacock. He watches events closely and approaches opportunities carefully, maintaining control over his roles without appearing to dominate situations. These features embody the successful hustler style which has come to be favored among young men in Port-of-Spain's streets. Often a man moves through periods of experimentation with bad john and saga boy postures while he is still young (as did Derek), but as he grows older he is very likely to become mellower, placing less emphasis on simple demonstrativeness and focusing instead on the subtleties of impression management and behavioral display, on the careful moves which are likely to lead to rewards in an adult world.

The major distinguishing feature of the hustler's "consciousness," if it can be called that, is his sense of superiority to mainstream, or "straight," life. Hustlers feel that their ability to sustain themselves through their hustles is infinitely preferable to the tedium of ordinary, disciplined work, especially when this work is to be found in a low-status and authoritarian context. And it is within such contexts that men such as these are apt to find the sorts of work available to them. The hustler feels that his design for living has more style and allows more expressive freedom than mainstream alternatives with their focus on the constraints of respectability and propriety. He knows, being poor and black, that plugging into mainstream circuits of thought and work will leave him at the very bottom rung of the ladder of success. He feels that his own style permits greater gracefulness and fluidity (or "cool") than he could achieve within the rigid confines of bourgeois norms of conduct. He sees himself as far better in survival skills; he is an operator, adept at manipulating opportunities for advantage and making the most out of very little. The hustler feels that his paramount concerns—getting high, involvement in music, commitment to certain sorts of "kicks," a diffused estheticism, contemplation and sociability—are highly preferable to the ordinary day-to-day concerns of the non-hustler, which revolve around achieving respectability and status in an authoritarian framework. Esthetic concerns must be emphasized here. In developing the rhythm of a conversation, in modulating speech, in moving the body in relation to others, in exploring and assessing textures of musical form, in gauging the tone of a drug-induced "high," in assembling an outfit for the day's liming, a concern with taste and style, with the esthetic contours of behaviors and settings, is always evident. The hustler, as Finestone put it describing the Chicago counterparts of Trinidadian limers, aims ". . . to contribute to a cultivated esthetic approach to living" (1964:285).

But the defining feature of a hustling lifestyle is the hustle itself, the choice of how to make a living, and how this choice affects the rest of one's time and concerns. The aim here is consistency: to seek a mode of making a living that dovetails with the ordinary day-to-day preoccupations of the hustler. Social scientists, and straight people in general, typically regard hustles as evasions of work, rather than as forms of work, and have assumed that hustles involve deception and, often, violence. Such a view distorts the reality of hustling as a mode of activity.

Hustlers *work* and often work hard; it is simply that the work they do is *viewed* as being illegitimate and therefore called something other than what it is: a way of making a living. While hustlers often like to brag that they can support themselves without "doing work" (they mean without being employed), and mainstream critics like to point to hustlers as easy opportunists (Are not all entrepreneurs opportunists?), hustlers seek work that insures some measure of freedom, a career of their own design and choice. When the hustler turns away from conventional work opportunities, he is saying that he would rather not work within a context where his actions and schedule are tightly monitored. Instead, he prizes personal control as essential to a successful hustling career. Hustlers often claim to admire Trinidad's "big boys," its leading entrepreneurs, because these men seem to be in control of their enterprises, rather than merely being cogs in the machinery. The hustler is unwilling to accept that powerless role, the typical place reserved for him in the socioeconomic system, just because he is black and poor. Submitting to such demeaning roles and functions is exceedingly distasteful to him. Derek expressed these feelings to me in a strident defense of his lifestyle:

> People ask me "what do I do"? They mean what's my job, what's my hustle. I tell them I'm just trying to live and they don't know what to say, what I mean. To them a man is seen as what he does— what his job is—that's all. That's what's wrong with this Trinidad society. Everybody is so concerned with position. Well, I hustle for my bread. A bourgeois man say, "look at them hustlers, they don't do anything, they aren't any good, man". But what do these people know. My hustle is part of me; I dig doing it and I feel free, it's me. Do you think I felt free working as a carpenter on some luxury house somewhere? Toiling away at some patio that a white man would use some day to drink tea and praise the Queen, doing that from morning to night, no man. I say live for what makes you feel good and deep, and make your work part of that. I don't want to

be one man during the day when I work, and something else when I come home at night. Let me be one thing and happy.

One Hustle: The Marijuana Trade

Becoming a marijuana trader was the favored hustle among such young Port-of-Spain men as Derek, Claudie and Catman for several reasons. First, it is clear that since the mid-1960s marijuana smoking has been steadily increasing in popularity as a mode of getting high, replacing alcohol for many Afro-American men. This popularity has generated a market and a demand. As demand has increased, involvement in the trade seems more and more alluring. Furthermore, participation in the marijuana trade finds the trader immersed in an ambience which he finds appealing and compatible with other values. Those who sell fake Omega watches to tourists care little for watches or tourists; prostitutes care little for sex with their clients. But the marijuana trader values his item of trade as much more than a salable commodity. Marijuana peddling (unlike peddling watches or cajoling tourists into listening to and paying for phony, lame Calypsos) is straightforward: the trader sells his product to those who want it. The hustler realizes that his customers know what they are buying and are able to gauge quality and market value. There is no trickery or chicanery here. Consequently, many men who are unwilling to engage in deceptive, underhanded hustles find marijuana trading a basically honest way of making a living.

Prestige attends those at the center of the marijuana distribution world. Those who buy and smoke marijuana value it highly, and they share this high regard with those who sell it to them. Can the same be said for the used car salesman, or a realtor passing off a shabby home as a treasure, or a wholesaler dealing off spoiled produce to retailers, or the distiller using glamorous advertising to increase rum sales? There is a world of difference between the attitude a man such as Derek has to the joint he is smoking and to the glass of rum in his hand. Rum is merely a way of getting high, loosening up, feeling good, and it has its ugly sides as well. But marijuana is more than just a cheap high; used respectfully it is seen as a pathway to insight and serenity. Marijuana users hold its traders in similar high regard. Furthermore, marijuana users view the mainstream culture's horror of marijuana and its portrayal of users with contempt. Therefore those who dare stand against mainstream critics and who flaunt their commitment in the face of shrill and threatening indictments are applauded and supported. From the ghetto point of view, the outsider's misunderstanding of marijuana is supremely ridiculous, mere confirmation of bourgeois rigidity and fixity, of a straight, European fear of ecstatic experience and imaginative flight. The idea that the marijuana trader is any worse a fellow that the dry goods merchant by virtue of the character of his trade simply makes no sense.

While marijuana use has an old history in Trinidad, dating from the chillum pipes and knowledge of cannabis cultivation that East Indians brought with them to the island in the 1850s, in recent years marijuana use has come to be associated with the Afro-American sector, and particularly with those blacks who feel deeply alienated from mainstream proprieties. The Rastafarians of Jamaica provide an even more extreme example of how commitment to marijuana use and repudiation of mainstream concerns with respectability becomes a clear-cut ideology. The ideology supporting marijuana use is partly an attempt to articulate a rebuttal to those who condemn this practice. Users are saying: your condemnations mean nothing to us; we celebrate our choices. In this sense, a sub-culture of opposition has developed around marijuana; its use is not merely an instrumental end, but a symbolic affirmation of culture-specific choices as against mainstream demands for conformity.

Apart from all this, marijuana traders also aim to be keen, opportunistic businessmen, ready to step in when advantage comes their way. And here consider Everett Hughes' reminder that "career" encompasses more than what we ordinarily mean by it; that deviant occupations, though they may accurately be called crimes, are also vehicles for the development of a career. The tone, sequencing, and progress of a career include a variety of work conditions and situations; acquisition of various skills; acquaintance with wide ranges of personnel and with modes of recruitment; and understanding of the special contingencies defining and promising success. Hustling, as a design for making a living within the confines of certain contingencies, resembles other careers, but it also differs significantly from many other kinds of work. Entry into hustling as a career does not normally require meeting rigid conditions established by colleagues or superiors. The hustler need not join a union, nor does he require job training, nor must he be licensed.

The marijuana trade in Trinidad has not been run from above, as it has elsewhere, and consequently no syndicate or similar structure determines the organization of the trade. Instead, patterns of trade have come to be established as various sorts of entrepreneurs positioned themselves here and there hoping to cash in on the increasing popularity of marijuana use; a pattern has evolved from the coalescence of ad hoc arrangements. I have alluded to facets of the marijuana trade and the character of traders above. Here I would briefly like to describe how traders operate, how marijuana trading exemplifies hustling as style and career, and how hustling in turn emerges from the special contingencies of street life.

In Port-of-Spain there is little sharp distinction between the wholesale and retail ends of the marijuana trade; the scale of trade was small enough in 1970 so that some measure of laissez-faire operation and free entry into the market exists. Wholesalers are simply those who sell marijuana to others who sell it to the consumer. Retailers sell directly to consumers. Most wholesalers are retailers as well, and many retailers turn to wholesaling if they can amass sufficient stakes. A rather small number of cultivators supply all the Port-of-Spain wholesalers; these cultivators are nearly all East Indians and grow their marijuana in isolated plots some distance from the city. The wholesaler is commonly a black man in his twenties or thirties: Derek, Claudie and Catman are examples. More likely than not the wholesaler knows nearly nothing about marijuana cultivation; this is strictly an Indian affair. Most wholesalers have several sources of supply. Sometimes wholesalers tend to deal exclusively with a single cultivator over a long period of time, but such an arrangement ultimately becomes transient and unreliable. Competition, as well as the frequency with which cultivators are arrested by the police, make it prudent for the wholesaler to diversify his sources of supply. Buying trips to cultivators tend to proceed as follows (excerpted from my field notes):

> Derek, Claudie and I drove with Carl to see Ramsingh, a grower
> located a few miles east of Rio Claro. Ramsingh was sitting around
> with a few of his sons and was quite cordial to Derek and the others.
> Derek asked to see what he had and one of Ramsingh's boys brought
> out a big burlap sack filled with marijuana. Derek took out a hand-
> ful and examined it carefully with a serious, skeptical, but inter-
> ested look on his face. Derek told Ramsingh that he thought this
> batch had quite a few twigs and leaves in it and not enough of the
> desirable resinous buds. Ramsingh shrugged and said this was all he
> had (actually, as Derek later acknowledged, what Ramsingh offered
> him was of rather good quality—something of which all parties were
> well aware—but Derek thought some active complaining might
> give him an edge in haggling). Ramsingh tore off a piece of brown
> paper bag and rolled a big "spliff" [a large marijuana cigar]. Derek
> and the others smoked this and, speaking discreetly among them-
> selves and not wishing to appear too eager in front of Ramsingh,
> commented on the excellence of the high. Derek asked about price
> and Ramsingh told him it was $100 per pound. Derek balked,
> complained, said it was good, but not *that* good and that the asking
> price was too steep. Ramsingh shrugged again and said that the price
> was fixed. Derek offhandedly asked him for three pounds and paid
> him $300.

This transaction was typical. There is always haggling but it is limited by standardized, and generally accepted, notions of fair price. And yet this is about the only link in the marijuana trade where there is any true "hustling," in the more usual sense of that term—where those in a transaction carefully adopt postures aimed to weaken the other's position in coming to terms on a deal.

Having made a purchase from a cultivator (usually under five pounds), the wholesaler returns to Port-of-Spain where he has already assembled a distribution network; if this is operating well, he has little trouble unloading his product. Many wholesale traders regard their work as a full-time vocation. Many others trade marijuana as moonlighters to supplement their income from other, frequently legal, occupations. Wholesalers prefer to limit themselves to wholesaling; this simplifies their involvements and reduces their exposure to police harassment. However, they are rarely able to limit their trade in this way because of the organization of marijuana trading centers, or "ghettos."

These ghettos are little urban niches—alleyways, back yards, bars, back rooms at gambling houses, residences—which are adequately insulated and yet sufficiently accessible to serve as centers for marijuana distribution. In 1971 there were perhaps a dozen major ghettos in the city and maybe two dozen smaller ones, along with innumerable "mini ghettos," little spots where wandering traders sold single marijuana cigarettes to passers-by. Typically, any one of these ghettos is dominated by one or two men who make it their center of operations. Ghetto bosses (such as Derek or Catman) normally have one or more young men or adolescents working for them. Such assistants are themselves frequently small-time retailers who make purchases from the wholesaler at low prices in return for small services they perform. Others serve as apprentices of sorts, acting as liaisons and liming with successful traders such as Derek in order to pick up on their savvy and knowledge.

A wholesaler returning from a purchasing trip with several pounds on hand prefers to divide his supply into one ounce lots and to sell these to retailers. But many retailers often lack the ten to fifteen dollars on hand to purchase an ounce and instead buy "parcels" and "half-parcels." A parcel of marijuana is a three-by-four inch brown paper envelope half filled with marijuana; a half-parcel is a somewhat smaller envelope also half filled. In 1971 a parcel sold for three dollars and a half-parcel for a dollar and a half. While some wholesalers shun parcel sales, most find themselves selling parcels with much greater frequency than ounces. At times a trader such as Derek is able to find clients who regularly buy ounces and he can limit himself to this unit of sale, but, with money as scarce as it is in the slums, wholesalers must be prepared to sell smaller units. All of this should indicate the miniature scale of the trade. Since the trade is exclusively domestic and since most buyers are poor black men, there is really very little room for big operators who can comfortably settle back into exclusive wholesaling. Most of the wholesalers know each other, at least by reputation, and they tend to cooperate as well as to compete. While every trader is interested in maximizing sales, each often finds it necessary to rely on others for supplies or information, as well as for tips on police actions. Altogether, then, the economic ambience is rather harmonious. This atmosphere exists in part because all wholesalers are also users. Howard Becker has argued that those labelled deviants (Port-of-Spain marijuana traders are an example) often cluster together under an umbrella of unity for protection and for cultural affirmation. The wholesaler is rarely able to spurn those who continually approach him for a "little bit of smoke." Such marijuana seekers are potential clients, and their visits are acknowledgments of the trader's reputation. Retailers are those who buy parcels and ounces from the larger traders and roll these into "sticks," or single marijuana cigarettes, for sale. There are all sorts of retailers serving a mixed clientele in a variety of locations.

At any given time, prices tend to be fairly standardized in Port-of-Spain. But prices do fluctuate, in a predictable fashion, throughout the year. Random fluctuations depend on the availability of supplies, as is true of other commodities. Occasionally when the police carry out a raid, especially a large, coordinated raid which nabs several growers, marijuana supplies may drop significantly, though usually only for a short time until purchasing and distribution adjustments can be made. When this happens prices increase. During the two months between Christmas and Carnival prices increase as well, reaching peaks just before Christmas and just before Carnival. During this "fête" season there is much greater demand for marijuana than is usually the case. The holiday season generates a great number of scenes where getting high is particularly appealing. Regular users increase purchases at this time, and those who normally do not use marijuana during the rest of the year sometimes make an exception during this festive time. Prices consequently increase with demand, and traders scramble furiously to acquire sufficient supplies to carry them through the active holiday season. Some traders hoard throughout the year so that they are adequately supplied during this period of heavy demand and high prices, and knowledge of hoarding is a great annoyance to customers who, seeking marijuana and knowing it is available, nevertheless cannot obtain it until the traders are willing to release it.

A purchaser wishing to buy marijuana may approach a trader if he knows him personally and, if not, he can go to one of the many ghettos in the city widely known as marijuana sales centers. If he is a regular user he is apt to be familiar with a number of such ghettos, and acquainted with some of the hangers-on who are affiliated with the traders who control sales there. These hangers-on serve as important liaisons between the traders and circuits of potential clients. A successful ghetto, such as Derek's was during most of my stay, is an active, busy place. Retailers stop in regularly to pick up supplies, exchanging joints and information. An ambience of sociability prevails.

Retailers who buy parcels, and sometimes ounces, from wholesalers roll these up into marijuana cigarettes and then either establish themselves at their own mini-ghettos—stoops or alleyways in their neighborhoods—or move from scene to scene on the lookout for potential clients.

A man who wishes to enter the marijuana trade must make himself and his intentions known to others, but he must not be so obtrusive as to encourage interference from the police or from other traders. Those who become successful traders are normally highly reputed men in their operational zones and are likely to have some good, reliable connections with wholesalers and with networks of potential clients prior to their engagement in the trade. The wholesale trader begins his career as a petty dealer, often serving as an assistant or a liaison working out of an established trader's ghetto. Many men, particularly young moonlighters who never aspire to rise above petty trading, are satisfied with this supplement to their other incomes. Others who do seek to rise in the trade build capital from their petty trading, establish their reputation and reliability in a chosen locale or among a circuit of customers, secure links with wholesalers and seek to learn something about contacting cultivators. Finally, they purchase a pound and establish their own ghettos. I accompanied Derek on several trips to cultivators where he was joined by two novice wholesale traders whom he brought along to introduce. Derek knew these men well and trusted them; they had been reliable clients and assistants and now wished to expand the scope of their trading and depended on Derek for help. Panhead had worked at Derek's ghetto for over a year, and one day he decided to move to San Juan, a proletarian suburb east of Port-of-Spain, and to set himself up there as a trader. He had learned the ins and outs of the trade working with Derek, and Derek in turn was happy to help Panhead in securing the necessary contacts. Such orientation and assistance is essential, since Port-of-Spain traders find themselves in a very alien world when they journey to East Indian rural districts in search of expectedly cautious and elusive cultivators. Links with cultivators must be secure if a trader is to become successful. Having continuous access to stock is often problematic, since cultivation is illegal and continual availability of supplies from a cultivator can never be assumed. The trader who fails to secure such links quickly loses clients because erratic supplies sends customers looking for more reliable sources.

In Port-of-Spain, then, one finds two sorts of marijuana traders: itinerant peddlers who sell sticks on the streets, and sedentary traders who work out of a permanent base of operations. Itinerant peddlers often aim to establish themselves as ghetto-based traders and work towards this end, echoing here the achievements of very different sorts of Trinidadian entrepreneurs—the Syrian merchants who began selling cloth door-to-door and wound up settled and established, with profitable enterprises. Both itinerant and sedentary traders operate quite successfully as the demand for marijuana increases steadily. The itinerant peddler finds clients at various social locales and occasions (liming on the streets, at musical events, in front of cinemas, at fêtes) where he feels there may be demand and where he finds that clients are happy to find it for sale. The settled trader is available to those who wish to obtain marijuana and are assured to know of a regular, dependable outlet.

Although the stakes are small in the marijuana trade, so are they in the legitimate occupational domains a proletarian man is likely to encounter. Marijuana trading can amount to a successful and satisfying career, enabling traders to earn as much as they would were they conventionally employed, and sometimes much more. Furthermore, the trader is in charge of his time and commitments and involves himself with an enterprise whose accoutrements he values. Those who wonder why men in depressed settings are often reluctant to seek legitimate employment and instead prefer to engage in illegal hustles should take this into account. On the other hand, the illegality of the marijuana trade and the pressures this imposes on traders make this a career which a potential trader is likely to approach with caution.

Attitudes to Marijuana

I offer two excerpts from my field notes to illustrate attitudes toward marijuana. First are Claudie's comments:

> Since we have the weed here things are different. People are cooler now. In the old days we had big gang riots and the steelband disturbances, and there was a lot of cutting up [slashing people with knives, usually strangers, for no other apparent reason than to leave a cut on their skins]. Not now. It has been the best thing to happen to Trinidad, this weed. There was a time when a middle-class person would not speak to someone like me; if I was little darker than you, you pretended you didn't know me. The weed has put much of a stop to this class and color thing. When we're all smoking together, you're not going to be concerned about my shade and where I am in the world. You take a middle-class boy who goes to the back of John-John, the really bad slum [a section of East Dry River], to smoke with the boys there. The next day he passes them on the road; he must talk to them. If you smoke with a man you and he have something going together, no matter what class he is.

And this from Catman:

> Weed has changed a number of things. I remember seven or eight years ago when I was still a boy, a teenager. Few of us used weed at that time and we all drank corn [rum]. At that time there was

always a lot of violence going about. Many of us would move around together, ready and nasty. We'd move from Basilon Street or Belmont to a theater in town or a fête in Laventille. We would be drinking and always ready to fight. Now I rarely see a fight taking place at a fête. With the weed, people have become cooler, easier to live with. They care less about who you are and where you belong. There was a time in Port-of-Spain when you and your partners stayed in the area and didn't move around too much. Because if you did—say, go to St. James—there would be some boys there ready to cut you up. And those boys from St. James stayed in St. James. They didn't come here, to East Dry River, because they knew if they did there would be trouble, they would return home damaged. Sometimes when a few partners were drinking and got to feeling tough we would move around the city looking for a fight. This is the way the steelbands worked [they were based in neighborhoods, stayed within them, and kept them clear of undesirable outsiders]. Now you walk where you want and don't worry. Because now people smoke and they are cooler. The reason all the Indians are still fighting all the time and we Creoles aren't, is because they still don't use the weed much. The ones who do look at the Indian bad johns and all their rum and violence as foolish; they lime with us.

These are ideological statements. They are designed to support a position and not merely to describe a reality. Nevertheless, they reflect commonly held views among young black men regarding the ambience and consequences of marijuana use. Observation and commentary both suggested to me that those who were increasingly drawn to marijuana use were shifting their style and commitments away from older patterns. Whereas in earlier years the saga boy style with its emphasis on flash and bravado dominated ghetto male imagery, a much more subdued style of presentation is characteristic of those in the marijuana world. "Cool heads" no longer spend so much money on clothes, a key expenditure in the saga boy style. They are now content to own a few pairs of blue jeans and an assortment of T-shirts, preferring to spend their money on marijuana rather than on ruffled shirts. Men of Carl's age and background, who are black and urban and cool, (but who have become cool only recently) are caught between the old style with its emphasis on flash and the new style with its focus on coolness, inner-directedness and introspection, unperturbability, spirituality and disdain for superficial demonstrativeness.

Mainstream condemnation of marijuana use has also contributed to the creation of a new subculture. That is, marijuana users are drawn to each other not only because they like to get high, but because outsiders label such activity as illegal and immoral, thereby drawing those who engage in it closer together in a protective and self-affirming circle of camaraderie. Initial assessments of strangers include determining whether they are smokers. More and more, one can assume that young, slum-based men are. For example, traders such as Derek, who routinely encounter police officers, are eager to discover whether a particular officer smokes, as many do. Although a trader never completely abandons caution before an agent of the law, he is likely to ease up if the police officer uses marijuana. Policemen, while continuing to arrest marijuana users and traders (though much less stringently than in the past), acknowledge that marijuana smoking has come to be linked with a reduction in violence, and often feel quite uncomfortable about the aspect of their work that has them coming down hard on marijuana users. I witnessed many occasions when off-duty police officers stopped by at Derek's ghetto to join him for a smoke.

For those within the marijuana subculture, harassment by mainstream enforcers seems arbitrary and vindictive. Why, they wonder, must they be punished for something so simple as "smoking the herb," while true abuses continue to flourish in Trinidadian society, unpunished and often celebrated.

Hustler Argot

Argot develops when a group of people sustains interpersonal relations centering around a specialized institution, activity or mode of action (a church, playing billiards, horseracing). Members who are involved in specialized activities or domains find they must make semantic distinctions far more intricate than those made by outsiders who are aware of the activity, but are not participants in its creation. A spectator at a game can usually make do with everyday, public language, but participants in the game are likely to need a much more exact lexicon in order to communicate about the game in a subtle, detailed fashion with other participants. Apart from this, members of specialized sub-groups use argot not only in order to communicate effectively among each other, but to set themselves apart from the outside world as specialists: the use of an argot serves to maintain boundaries and to delimit membership to insiders. Furthermore, argot may serve as a private language that allows insiders to shield their activities or their intentions from interfering outsiders. Typically, hustlers use a variety of terms and references to talk to each other about scenes and actions which are mysterious to non-hustlers, or at least to people who are set distantly apart from the hustling world.[8] Argot adds a technical lexicon to everyday speech in order to facilitate communication among its speakers and to maintain boundaries between those speakers and outsiders. Some argot terms distinguish insiders from outsiders; others refer to special techniques and operations that interest insiders and must be obscured from outsiders. Argot terms are used to signify the special and outstanding qualities of members and their lives, and to enhance an *esprit de corps,* emphasizing the solidarity of the "we." Among marijuana users the concealment function of argot use is especially apparent, as when traders use argot terms when making a transaction in public in order to conceal the nature of their business.

Hustling: An Overview

From the point of view of mainstream rules of conduct, the hustler is doubly a violator. First, he transgresses conventional notions of morally acceptable behavior. He is viewed as wily and manipulative and this goes against the grain of idealized (though, of course, unrealized) mainstream beliefs about the sorts of proprieties which are appropriate to personal dealings among people. Secondly, he makes his living in unconventional ways which in their very success threaten the integrity of bourgeois standards. If his hustle happens in some ways to be illegal, as most are, he violates legal rules as well as conventions. Straight people often believe that hustlers victimize innocent others, when in fact most of their clients (those who buy drugs, pay for sex, wish to gamble) seek their services.

For their part, hustlers regard these condemnations as nothing so much as illustrations of the hypocrisy underlying mainstream values. The stigma of mainstream critics only scores them points in their own social circles, and they hold the self-righteousness of critics in contempt. Hustlers recognize the potential of outsiders (especially in legal guise) to harass them, and try to protect themselves. But, as Polsky puts it, the hustler is ". . . segregated not only from his 'betters' but from their opinions of him" (1967:65). Among poor black people, even those who are straight, the hustler's concerns are tolerated and widely accepted as understandable responses to slum conditions.

There is another side to all this. In a social setting marked by poverty, where some choose to make their living in ways deemed illegal, trouble arises continually. Much of this trouble emerges from the dangers inherent in illegal work and the caution this requires. But trouble comes from internal considerations as well: competition, the potential for violence, the sometimes fragile qualities of friendship. Several men at a party mistake Carl for a bad john they are looking for, someone who held up a card game. They smash several rum bottles over his head and Carl winds up in the hospital with a concussion and deep cuts. One of Slats' assistants, a man he particularly trusted, steals a large amount of marijuana from him. Certainly he can't report the theft to the police. Slats searches for the man and meanwhile has to worry about not having yet paid his supplier for the stolen marijuana. Derek and Claudie share their income, with one or another holding on to their common "bread" at any given time. But one day Claudie decides to take the money and, together with Rat, purchase a number of cassette tape recorders. A series of mishaps occur, they lose the money, and Derek realizes there is no way of getting his half back from Claudie. Their relationship, previously the epitome of close friendship, cools off and Claudie leaves the house for a while. Dum-Dum smashes up Carl's Renault while he is out hunting down one of his women. The car belongs to Carl's employer and Carl loses his job. Jennifer, a prostitute, is thrown out of the particularly lucrative club at which she normally works after permitting a man to convince her to leave the club with him for an evening, a violation of the rules. Derek goes out with a woman who, as it turns out, had been previously attached to a jealous and ill-tempered bad john in Belmont. This man, together with several friends, find Derek and beat him. Derek takes it as part of life and shrugs it off as a misfortune. A week later they attack him for a second time. The third time he encounters several of them at a bar in his own familiar territory. They again begin taunting him, but this time he grabs for an axe and chops one of the men over the head, nearly killing him.

Trouble is endemic in the streets. While rapport, camaraderie, and cultural tightening in response to mainstream antagonisms are characteristic of the lives of the black poor in the slums of Port-of-Spain, trouble arises out of difficulties of making-do and establishing security. Of course this is the main focus of middle-class critics who seize upon such aspects and magnify them into what they claim is the essential and distinctive ambience of lower-class life.

City life for poor, black Trinidadians is neither paradise nor hell. Lifestyles reveal the variety of distinctive responses which the poor and black have made over the decades and centuries to conditions imposed upon them by the greedy ambitions of others. In this chapter I have chosen to focus on those responses most critical of mainstream values and most revealing of cultural alternatives.

Chapter 4

Black, Poor, and Male in Trinidad

We may regard a set of activities as comprising an institution, or as being institutionalized when the patterns of behavior such a set encloses are directed to fundamental and perennial concerns of social life. Institutions entail the ordering of behavior in persistent and continuous patterns so as to sustain the satisfactory operations of fundamental activities. Such patterns are normative and are supported by sanctions. We may also see institutions as "spheres"—ranges of activity which seem to have something to do with each other, and which are enduring and continuous.

This is what we mean when we speak of the economy, or religion, or the family as institutions. These are ranges of activity and patterns of behavior directed to the support of some fundamental sphere of social operations. We identify general institutional spheres such as "the economy" or "religion" as characteristic of all social life and reflective of perennial human concerns; and we seek to specify the historical and ecological designs of these institutions. Hence we speak of the "Tikopian economy" and "Nuer religion." One can pick up few ethnographies that do not take institutional sorting out for granted, and we expect chapters on kinship, politics, religion, and so forth.

But institutional analysis becomes tricky for at least two different reasons. First, there is again the problem of reification. When we encapsulate a sphere of social life or a range of activities as an institutional domain, we paint a border around such a sphere or range, fixing it as a "thing" in the social world. Leach and others have repeatedly pointed out the dangers of this effort, and shown how conceiving society in terms of certain conventional institutional structures (such as lineages) has predetermined the shape of inquiry, constraining attempts at imaginative analysis (Leach 1962). Institutional analysis often leads to taxonomic overspecification. We are made to feel that a society is composed of institutions, returning to the fundamental problem of the organismic metaphor of functionalism.

Nonetheless, we cannot escape the utility of institutional analysis. While only action is real and concrete, institutional frames allow us to grasp sequences of action and to see how they are patterned. And here a second problem arises. Our informants also think along institutional lines. They too demarcate ranges of activity and reify them as spheres. Both ordinary Trinidadians and I, the ethnographer, were able to talk about such things as "the Roman Catholic Church" or "the law." But ethnographers' and informants' understandings and assessments of institutional spheres may not correspond, and it is important to gauge ethnographic representations of institutions against those of our informants. We may be seeing a forest; they may only be seeing trees. Middle-class Trinidadians view much of what I have described in the previous chapter as crime, though from the inside it looks like work. For the anthropologist both assessments are real and important. While trading in marijuana is work and career for Derek, it is crime and sin for others. We have to grasp differences of points of view among a population and see how the definitions these points of view inspire lead to a dialectic of struggle over how social life is construed. We do not take in behavior cold; we frame it. Social experience unfolds in an arena of multiple frames, the ethnographer's among them. And particularly in a complex society such as Trinidad, this arena becomes a place for combat and competition.

So while institutional analysis often serves to clarify the patterns and events of social life, it may obscure them as well. We have to remain fluid and flexible here, considering "emic" or native assorting of social life as well as the manner in which we have come to assort it. It is necessary to remain continuously on guard, as Leach has urged, and question the validity and usefulness of various institutional enclosures. Patterns abstracted from the observation of concrete behavior and events are influenced by the sorts of institutional frames applied to them, and so we must be always conscious of these frames, matching them against our experience and continually judging their value.

Studies of the social life of the poor, especially in complex, polyethnic urban settings, have emphasized the relationships between the distinctive features of lower-class sociocultural styles and the wider society to which these features are (or are not) linked. A major assumption in many of these studies has been that *alienation* from dominant cultural and behavioral motifs—from mainstream values, rules, behaviors, possibilities—lies at the heart of the culture of the poor in bourgeois societies. In regard to an assessment of Afro-American life, there are a number of more particular arguments. One view has claimed that poor, black men are alienated from certain kinds of experiences and social possibilities, especially those concerning stable family life and employment (Liebow 1967, Valentine 1968). These men are so alienated not because they reject mainstream social and cultural possibilities, for in fact they find them quite attractive. But they are able to predict that in the course of their lives, and in the lives of those like them, any sustained attempt to achieve such goals will likely result in failure. That is, the mainstream world, represented by such values as stable employment and an orderly family life, rejects them; they do not reject it. The analyses proceeding from these assumptions have tended to focus on those crucial junctures where failure occurs—the points at which the poor encounter mainstream ideals and expectations and the grim consequences of these encounters: resignation, cynicism, rootlessness, hopelessness, fatalism.

Such an orientation is certainly a healthy counterpoint to an earlier view which drew an image of a social Darwinist struggle in which the ancestors of the poor lost out in the past, and their descendents consequently find themselves immobilized in their unenviable positions. Such a view is typical of critics who have consistently been enemies of the poor and have busied themselves weaving theories and assembling arguments to justify their antago-nism. It is also not surprising that such critics, with their deficient ideas but attractive politics, have come to dominate much of the thinking behind policy-making that affects the poor. Daniel Moynihan and Edward Banfield are examples.

But the stress on failure, while correctly pointing to the intrinsic relation-ship between poverty and oppression, has led to a rather empty picture of what alienated, jobless and unattached men do with their lives. In the previous chapter I sought to flesh out this picture, a necessary task if the poor are to appear as anything but victims, grim shadows of social defeat. This effort requires a renewed interest in the *culture* of the poor.

Much of the recent progressive work in urban anthropology and sociology has aimed to dismantle Oscar Lewis's assertions about the "culture of poverty." Lewis's critics have complained that his concern with culture, and the bleak picture he has painted of the culture of the poor, reflect a mis-directed emphasis on the *specificity* of poor people's cultural styles as against those of the wider society. Lewis, they claim, conveys an impression that proletarian culture is a malignant, regrettable consequence of continuous social defeat. Failing to gain access to mainstream orbits of success and achievement, the poor retreat to marginal adaptations and outlooks that become fixed as enduring cultural patterns and only increase their vulner-ability. Narrowing the debate to the Afro-American poor, critics such as Valentine accept Lewis's assessment of the social circumstances of poverty, but reject his claim that such circumstances have generated a *distinctive* cultural response, and a pathological one at that. Instead, they argue, blacks have for the most part accepted mainstream cultural perspectives, but are unable to transform the imperatives of such perspectives into concrete social achievements. The poor are continually frustrated in their attempts to turn aspirations into realities. As so often happens in the social sciences, this has become an "either/or" debate: either the poor share mainstream aspirations but cannot achieve the standards of living which these aspira-tions presuppose; or, facing enduring and oppressive social conditions, they retreat to a defeatist culture incapable of amelioration.

It may very well be true that Lewis, in his journeys through urban Mexico and Puerto Rico, came upon distinctive and negative worldviews, subcultures whose design reflected social impotence and fatalism. It is pointless for critics such as Valentine, from their North American (and Afro-American) vantage points, to insist that Lewis was wrong. On the other hand, Valentine and others are probably correct in their claims that many North American blacks largely share mainstream cultural models of "ought," adopting these as goals and seeking to design lifestyles in accordance with their prescriptions.

The difficulty with this debate is once again the tendency to reify culture; to find a *something* ("the poor," "black Americans") to enclose within a cultural skin. In regard to the relationship between culture and social behavior, I think one can accurately make at least this claim: when, over succeeding generations, people modify their behavioral options in accordance with situational and environmental demands, it is very likely that their cultural styles—shared and conventionalized designs for living—will be modified as well. Hence we must speak in terms of specific modifications that reflect historically shared experience, social change among Afro-Trinidadians, for example; and avoid ahistorical generalities, such as the culture of "blacks" or "the poor." It may be that Puerto Rican slum dwellers have developed maladaptive designs for living, suitably conceived of as a culture of poverty; and it is equally possible that blacks in Washington, D.C. largely remain committed to mainstream values and middle-class aspirations. Only if one reduced both Puerto Rican slum dwellers and Washington blacks to examples of a single category, "the poor," can one conduct a debate. Such reductionism is invalid, and consequently the debate is pointless.

My concern here is to consider the links between styles of culture ("models of" and "models for," in Geertz's terms) and styles of social behavior and organization in Trinidad. Certainly there are many variations in the way that lower-class cultural styles are linked to lower-class social conditions. Here I seek to address only Trinidadian variants. Culture is best viewed as an historical repertory of options woven into particular patterns, more like a tapestry than a system. The task then is to examine these particular tapestries—to reveal the variations in ambience.

The problem is this: why is it that in Trinidad, as in so many other Caribbean societies, mainstream assumptions about how life should be designed and what sorts of commitments it should include are supported by what is commonly a very small middle-class, rather than by the masses of peasants and proletarians who make up the majority of the population? Phrased another way, this question is a critique of the arguments made in the previous chapter. How is it possible to claim that the rules and values supported by a small and often self-insulated portion of a population may be viewed as a mainstream? What does it really mean to describe deviants from such a mainstream, when these deviants amount to a large part, even a majority of the population? David Lowenthal obliquely suggested why this may be so when he wrote: "Other countries have minority problems, but in the West Indies the 'minority' is a numerical majority and the whole flavor of affairs derives from this fact" (1967:585). That is, cultural dominance is not a reflection of sheer numbers; the black and Indian poor may amount to the overwhelming bulk of the population, but they are not dominant and their intentions do not prevail. Cultural dominance is intertwined with political structure, and here we must begin to speak of a politics of culture.

Quite simply, in the Caribbean politically powerful and usually white bourgeoisies have laid down the rules, invoking and enforcing those rules through the schools, churches, courts, newspapers. This elite had imposed a cultural design—what I have been calling a mainstream—upon a politically subordinate black majority. In many ways this imposition has been effective, but it has also faced strong resistance. Such antagonisms and contradictions are characteristic of the culturally complex ambience of a society such as Trinidad. Against the intrusion of Euro-Caucasian demands, the Afro-American spirit—what has best been phrased as "soul"—has pressed its own internal demands and striven for its own integrity. On this cultural battlefield have arisen a number of stylistic responses.

Through its vehicles of instruction and control (the court, the pulpit, the classroom, the barracks), the dominant elite for centuries has had the opportunity to shape the poor into an image of its choice. To some extent this process has succeeded, many of the black poor have adopted such an image as their own. But there have been various distortions as well. What the poor who are positively attuned to mainstream proprieties so often manage to achieve is a *caricature* of mainstream success, not having sufficient resources to realize their goals completely. In Trinidad such mainstreamers are associated with "white" behavioral styles which gain much of their shape through the contrasts drawn by condemning "black" styles as inferior. And here, then, is the bitter irony: the servant who adopts his master's cloak of respectability. But this cloak is a garment worn to insulate its wearer from the historical reality of his past. Nothing disheartened me more in Trinidad than to hear a poor man of African origin speak blissfully of the tastefulness and graciousness of whites, particularly the British, while mocking and belittling those who share his origin for their "low-class" ways: praising the Queen and condemning the "riffraff" of the streets.

More commonly, acceptance of mainstream codes is much more tentative and irregular, and these codes are "stretched," as Rodman puts it (1970:194ff), to accommodate the reality of shifting social circumstances. Mainstream options are only part of the available repertory of cultural choices; other options stem from continuing class and ethnic commitments, as well as from the changing contingencies of everyday experience. Behavioral strategies pivot around guidance provided by mainstream codes as to the "oughts" of life, together with ad hoc accommodations reflecting internal conditions and sentiments. The culture of poor blacks in Trinidad, then, is an orbit of possibilities with dual traditions, one European and the other African. And these traditions have been modified and continuously readjusted in light of unique Trinidadian circumstances, yielding as an outcome a Creole society with plural threads.

These people pay lip service to marriage as the correct form of family union, but reality often urges more flexible and tentative common-law arrangements. Most are affiliated with one or another Christian churchs, but syncretic, distinctly Trinidadian religious variants incorporating African stylistic themes tend to be more compelling for many believers. The universe of work is inescapable, but many regard ghetto-specific alternatives, such as those described in the previous chapter, as legitimate possibilities. There is participation in the political bureaucracy, but local, rejectionist politics have developed at the same time. Cosmopolitan (European) culture is given a nod of respect, but local esthetic creations rooted stylistically in African antecedents are preferred. Material concerns preoccupy the poor, as they preoccupy all in a bourgeois society, but a long tradition of deprivation has also suggested the danger of materialist aspirations, and the importance of mutually sustaining social rapport.

Poor blacks in Trinidad feel the continual necessity of manipulating possibilities and using cultural resources to maximize aims and intentions. Trinidadians are aware of a wide repertory of sociocultural choices, and are confronted with a variety of often contradictory options regarding what sorts of goals they should seek. They act selectively and opportunistically, for the most part, rather than strictly following the letter of any particular cultural code. Rather, they seek fluid social arrangements and the many options that accompany such constantly shifting circumstances.

The repertory of options and resources *is* limited, but it is much broader and more flexible than outsiders often imagine. While it is certainly true that black people, especially when they are poor, are cut off from possibilities available to others, they design new possibilities and discover new options—they turn to internal resources, thereby augmenting their limited access to mainstream opportunities and creating unique alternatives.

In this book I have tended to focus on those who feel hostility or ambivalence toward mainstream notions of what constitutes acceptable conduct and outlooks. These men are hardly cut off from mainstream orbits of influence; it is in the nature of Caribbean society that such orbits should continually intrude on their lives. But they are aware of the contradictions between mainstream and distinctly ghetto styles and, cementing their loyalties and commitments, lean toward ghetto styles while spurning mainstream demands. These men know there is much to be gained from occasionally bowing in the direction of the mainstream, but they are also aware that to do so compromises the ghetto styles to which they are committed.

Work

Suffice it to say that employment possibilities have been very limited in Trinidad for urban black men, and the work that has been available has generally been tedious and often demeaning. All Trinidadians are quite aware of this and offer a variety of comments. Aston, a chronic downtown limer, had this to say:

> You look at a limer like me. People see me hanging around and they say, "Why isn't he working?" Well, it's true that there's unemployment and you can't get jobs too easily these days. But what about me? I can work. I could find myself a job this afternoon. But why should I? What will it mean? Taking in a few dollars a week, maybe a hundred a month. And where is that going to get me? Sure, people are trying to get jobs, and I'd be the first to work and to work hard if you made it worth my while. And that goes for most of the fellows I lime with. But until something good comes along—and I don't see it coming—I'm just going to stay "unemployed." Why should I break my back for nothing?

Such cynicism should not be at all surprising. This man has assessed the possibilities and found them to be slim indeed. He has nothing against working per se, but he is not about to take a job merely for the sake of being employed, thereby pleasing others whose standards are not his own. He survives very nicely for the time being, hustling in a small way, and he has put out of his mind those aspirations that it requires money and security to achieve. Rat voiced an even more cynical attitude:

> People are saying, "Look at those young men and boys in Laventille. What they need is jobs. You give them jobs and they'll become respectable. Work hard and may be able to make it to Diego Martin one of these days." Well, the way I look at it, there's nothing so splendid about working. I'm interested in "living," man. And living to me doesn't mean working for some racist honky boss for nothing. Tell you the truth, I'm happy liming. I'm happy just staying cool and getting on. You hustle a little, you've got friends, maybe some family, you can live. Life doesn't mean sacrificing myself to endless years of "employment" [said with deep scorn], toiling. I'm interested in developing myself, developing my mind. Maybe it's too

late for me. I wish I had stayed in school and got on better there.
But you'd be surprised how much I learn about life just standing
around, liming and watching the world pass by. Much more than I
would digging ditches from dawn to dusk for a couple of dollars.

These men are stressing not only the inadequacies of available work, but
they are denying a desire for conventional employment. Rat is not willing
to work at degrading and unrewarding jobs; rather than viewing unemployment as a problem, a shortcoming or a mark of defeat, he sees it as linked
to his freedom. Unemployment implies available time, time to be filled
with inquiry, action, and contemplation. Rat is one of a large number of
young Trinidadians who have not merely lamented the country's employment situation as it affects them, but have gone on to question the nature
of employment itself in a bourgeois society. As they see it, the only rewards
of work in a bourgeois society are cash and, possibly, power. Since the work
available to them offers little opportunity for gaining either, work itself
comes under attack; it is a constraint rather than an opportunity. The linkage
between work—holding down a steady job—and respectability has far less
meaning for the young than for their mainstream—oriented parents. The
young are more politically and ideologically sensitized: they question, among
other things, the validity of the assumption that to be an adult requires holding on to a steady job. They are aware that this assumption is put forth by
those who are most concerned with social order and the maintenance of the
status quo. A seasoned limer, a friend of Derek's, had this to say, putting
such attitudes in a wider perspective of class and ethnicity:

People say, "Look at the Indians, look at the Chinese, look at the
Syrians, look at the Portuguese. They've worked hard and now
they've made it. They're on top now. Look down the road. See all
those shops—Chinese and Indian and Syrian and Portuguese." And
then they say, "look at the Negro. Where are his shops? He came
here first and still he's on the bottom. I guess he just doesn't know
how to handle a business. He doesn't know how to run one, how to
make and manage his money." Well, my answer is that all these
critics are fools. They're mouthing nonsense. See that Chinese
shop [he points to a typical Chinese grocery down the street]? That
fellow works all day long. He works hard and he's been working hard
all his life. He's saved his few pennies and he has his little shop.
He's a businessman. You can say the same thing about the Indian.
He works like a slave. He doesn't spend money. He grows his bit of
rice. He buys his bit of land. He saves and saves and saves. See, the
Indian's made something out of himself. You know what I have to
say about all that: so what? They're not "successful" in my eyes.
What are they saving for? What are they sacrificing themselves for?

For some small business which brings them hardly anything, just so they can say that they "own" it. I say they're fools. They're wasting away their lives. You only have one life to live. I don't understand it. Why live if your life is one endless sacrifice? So the Negro may not own too many businesses, and he may not be making too much money. But he can breathe and he can feel. He isn't just an adding machine like those coolie and Syrian bastards who care only about what they can squeeze out of you.

Here cynicism is joined by bitterness. This man knows all too well that the finger of accusation is always pointed at black men like himself, contrasting them with members of other ethnic groups who are claimed to have "made it." He takes a stand. Why, he asks, is a toiling commitment to success at work and money-making any more commendable than an attempt to lead a life of leisure and feeling? Why is pleasure scorned and sacrifice applauded?

Others are less strident in their antagonism toward mainstream concerns. They express equal measures of commitment and ambivalence to those concerns. The following excerpt comes from a typically long monologue by Reds Sullivan about the nature of life and work in Trinidad. Reds has been quite successful in holding down a good job, but he has also been strongly drawn to the free and easy liming life of the streets. Reds rarely exempted himself from his gentle, fatalistic criticisms, and he phrased much of the following to apply to himself as well:

The Negro won't work for anything if he can get it without effort. There are two things the black man in Trinidad doesn't like: work and violence. Here people go to a boss, curse him up and down, sneer at him and then ask him for a raise. But don't ask them to work. A man working here in Trinidad—if he puts in four hours of work in an eight-hour day, that's very unusual. Two hours would be more like it. This is especially true of the civil servant. The civil servant goes to work in the morning, and right away goes to the toilet and locks himself up with a newspaper. In the United States a man is expected to work a full day for his pay. He gets time for a cigarette but if he just loafs around, he's out. In Trinidad a man takes off some time for lunch, goes to a bar to spend a few hours, drinks a few cold beers, has a few good belches, checks out all his friends, finds out about any fêtes coming up, and when he's all done he decides there's no point going back to work since it's already so late, so he just splits for home. Then the next day the guy tells you he wants $500 a month. You take a man in Trinidad who's poor, he may be poor but he eats three good meals a day, he's got a TV, things aren't all that bad. In other countries, if a man is really poor he's willing to fight, to give up his life in a struggle. Not in Trinidad. People here just love life too much. They'd rather live real poorly than get themselves into a jam where they may be in danger. That's why there never will be a revolution in Trinidad. The people may listen to you, they may say "That boy's got some good ideas," and they may vote you in, but if you ask them to take up arms, forget it. Nobody's going to risk getting hurt. No one's going to take politics *that* seriously. Here in Trinidad if people hear some dog fussing up in a trash bin, making a little bit of noise, they all hide under their beds. Everyone just wants life to be nice and easy—no troubles, you know. But then again the Trinidadian always seems to know how to get by, how to make it in a tough world. If not this way then that way, always ready to try out different things. He loves his freedom. He'd rather do it his way than to be told "you *must* do it this way." When they come down here from Barbados they don't understand that. How easy going the Trinidadian is. Bajans have been used to listening to the boss and doing what they're told. Trinidadians are always thinking about how to get past the boss. How to get by without pressure. Man, they *hate* pressure.

This is one man's caricature of the Trinidadian social scene, particularly as it relates to attitudes toward work. Reds's comments are especially interesting because, through their chastisements and apologies, they reveal the very mixed bag of attitudes Trinidadians commonly express about themselves as a population. Mainstreamers like to condemn those who do not work as lazy good-for-nothings who have not come under the influence of such sobering institutions as the church and the family. The excerpts which precede Reds's statement provide a vigorous response to such an indictment, turning it around, and directing it back at the smugness of mainstream values. Reds's statement suggests a middle ground, incorporating a variety of attitudes, and pointing a critical finger inward and outward. He chastizes black Trinidadians for what he claims is their casual, uncommitted approach to work and social improvement, as well as their lack of political courage. But his criticism also contains an edge of oblique respect and admiration for the savvy Trinidadians have shown in their ability to remain optimistic and cleverly manipulative under trying circumstances.

Reds asks a favorite Trinidadian question, "Why is it that we Trinidadians cannot make progress and improve our personal and social conditions?" The answer, "We are unwilling to take the work of change seriously, and to cooperate responsibly for purposes extrinsic to our personal satisfactions." But when he compares Trinidadians with those who are reputedly serious in their commitments to work (those from Barbados, for example, for there are many migrants from that island working in Trinidad), the Trinidadian style of hedonism and everyday resourcefulness is compared favorably with populations who "do not really know how to live." With his mainstream hand, Reds points an accusing finger at the irresponsibility he feels is characteristic of much of the national style; but with his other, he gently mocks this attitude, and subtly displays his pride in a people who he feels are experts at evasion. Here he expresses a distinctly ghetto value: manipulating available possibilities in order to maximize personal freedom and satisfaction. This ability, or adaptive style, is felt by both blacks and others to apply specifically to the Afro-American sector. This is in part yet another example of a rather offhanded attribution of characteristics to an ethnic group. But a more general truth is contained here. The black adaptive style *is* special and its distinctiveness reflects the very special history of Afro-Americans—a history of slavery and oppression. In the context of such experience, there arose widespread alienation from mainstream notions about the desirability of putting in one's share as a responsible citizen, particularly when this responsibility implied having to do miserable work for next to nothing, which it usually did and still does.

Alienation has generated behavior and attitudes which emphasize avoidance and manipulation as strategies to sustain the continually threatened freedoms of the Afro-American proletariat, allowing its members to make out as best as they can in a world which holds out few material rewards and insists on erecting barriers to their advancement.

For example, as slaves and then later as freed men and women, blacks were discouraged from engaging in entrepreneurial activities. The destructive consequences of slavery and the post-slavery period conditioned a black population which became atomized, geographically mobile, poor, and cynical. As slaves and then again as wage earners, blacks found few opportunities to become effective decision makers in their economic lives. Decisions were, and still are, typically made for them. This is not to claim that the social lives of slaves were empty or that they were unable to develop useful economic skills. On the contrary, the very difficulties of the slave experience made black people invent adaptive skills to stretch the very limited resources available to them. But the contingencies of the slave system did imply that slaves did not usually engage in activities involving long-range social and economic planning.

As a consequence, freed slaves encountered the postslave experience with a particular set of outlooks that differed significantly from those of other ethnic groups brought to Trinidad to replace the now emancipated slaves as plantation workers. Furthermore, these new groups, the Chinese and Indians, very much in contrast to African slaves, were permitted to retain much of their sociocultural coherence, and did not face the sorts of impediments to social activity and flexibility that slavery imposed and assumed. Most importantly, these groups did not face the disruption of family life as did African slaves, whose traditional family and social ties were broken and rearranged to facilitate the needs of the plantation system. This, especially, had an effect on the cultural preparedness required to successfully engage in entrepreneurial activities. Most particularly, other ethnic groups have succeeded in business by mobilizing family labor. In the cohesive ambience of the Chinese or Indian or Syrian family, kin were drawn together into cooperative units to fuel successful enterprises. Such families usually relied on outside labor only when an enterprise began to grow beyond the capacities of family-supplied efforts. Everyone endured and sacrificed together, and success often emerged just because the family supplied labor, thereby keeping costs down. Such a strategy was never available to Afro-Americans. Among blacks the family has been a looser, more flexible orbit of kin-based relationships. This, as I have briefly argued earlier, has provided blacks with certain adaptive advantages, but it has precluded the sort of capacity to organize on-going enterprises as family projects which has been possible for those populations where family groups tended to be tightly drawn together.

The position of blacks in Trinidad has been, first and foremost, proletarian. After slavery, they became wage earners and innumerable barriers hindered their economic success. There has never been a viable black peasantry as there has been an Indian one. Indians, by owning and cultivating land and by selling crops in the marketplace, gained decision-making experience, entrepreneurial talents and capital. Experience and resources together allowed them to expand their participation in the commercial life of the island as a local white economic elite waned in importance. Furthermore, various ethnic groups often have special economic needs (such as East Indian foods and Indian cinema) which businessmen from these groups are likely to service. Such culturally-specific markets are normally closed to outsiders. In contrast, black consumers have typically patronized businessmen from ethnic groups other than their own.

A unique set of conditions, then, established a cultural groundwork which made it exceptionally difficult for blacks to gain entry into the entrepreneurial domain. The social consequences of slavery generated a role for the Afro-American limited to wage labor at menial work. Meanwhile, other ethnic groups were developing and carving up entrepreneurial domains and the "colored" middle class moved toward the professions. Blacks in Trinidad have found themselves funneled into brittle economic positions. Attitudes toward work must be understood against this background.

Class and Ethnicity

Nearly all the movie theaters in Port-of-Spain are divided into three sections. Tickets to the *balcony* section are most expensive, and this is where all white and middle-class patrons sit. Occasionally there is a poor, ghetto couple here, their choice of seats reflecting the occasion of a special date. There is almost never any noise in this part of the theater, and the patrons who select these seats disdain those in the more rowdy sections of the cinema. The *house* usually includes the back half of the orchestra section; tickets are less expensive than for the balcony, and the audience here is mixed, though most of the poorer, black patrons sitting here are single women, couples or the elderly. The *pit* is the front half of the orchestra, and contains seats considerably shabbier than those elsewhere in the theater but also considerably cheaper. While there is a common entrance for those who purchase balcony and house tickets located at the front of the theater—near the rest rooms and next to the nicer refreshment stands—there is a separate entrance to the pit at the rear. This entrance is usually a single, narrow door, making entry into the cinema very uncomfortable for pit patrons. Inside the theater there is a physical barrier between the house and pit sections which is intended to prevent patrons sitting in the pit from climbing over into the house and bothering the patrons there. The composition of the pit is nearly exclusively black, male, poor and young. Women rarely sit in this section, and a man who would normally choose to sit here when alone will buy house seats if he is accompanying a woman. One never sees a white or Chinese moviegoer in the pit, and rarely an East Indian. The pit audience tends to interact with the film, much to the annoyance of those in other sections who are there to watch; the pit audience is raucous and continually on the lookout for double-entendres.

This arrangement of Port-of-Spain cinemas partly imitates British models where the balcony is viewed as the most choice and most expensive seating location, while the front of the orchestra is seen as the least desirable and cheapest. Adopting this seating model, Trinidadians arrange themselves into these sections on the basis of class and ethnicity. Attending the cinema is one of the very few occasions when whites and other members of the social elite find they must share a zone of participation with the black males for whom they have so much contempt and whom they tend to fear. An exceptional social moment occurs at the end of a film when pit patrons, rather than waiting endlessly to exit through the one small pit exit door, jump the railing and join the rest of the patrons in exiting from the theater. Here is a mingling of the kind carefully avoided by Trinidad's bourgeois citizens. And here one sees how a powerless class has come to be able to intimidate a powerful elite—a microcosmic moment for Trinidadian social history.

This stratification of places of entertainment and sport is common in Port-of-Spain. One sees it at cricket matches, at various shows during Carnival and elsewhere. In regard to cinemas, again, not only are particular theaters divided into clearly delineated spatial sections reflecting socioeconomic divisions, but cinemas themselves vary according to class. The theaters divided as above are the "better" cinemas, in that they are where middle-class people are willing to go. But of course the poor are just as eager to see the current, well-projected films screened at these theaters, and so the audiences, much to the chagrin of bourgeois viewers, are always highly mixed. People speak of "first," "second," and "third" class cinemas. A third-class theater is one where there are "a lot of noisy scamps" in attendance, as bourgeois patrons would tell you, and where what the culture brokers consider to be low-grade action films are shown.[10] A first-class theater tends to be located in somewhat better sections of town and shows "classy" films such as British historical dramas, *The Sound of Music* and so forth.

I offer the Trinidadian cinema as an example of how class related sociospatial arrangements come to characterize social scenes. Going to the movies in Port-of-Spain, as is true of participation in any other mixed sort of event, reveals the residues of Trinidadian social history in action. At events such as these people mingle, but class and ethnic divisions markedly punctuate this mingling. Such punctuations are generally characteristic of Trinidadian social life.

Two key features stand out in Trinidad's social history. The first is the succession of ethnic groups that entered the island as the plantocracy required their labor. Secondly, the rationale behind the island's development was, first and foremost, to seek profits from the exploitation of agricultural resources and, more recently, from petroleum resources. Of course this rationale has required extensive human exploitation in the form of capitalist institutions and a class-based system of social stratification has developed as well. Class and ethnicity, then, stand out as the two most important markers in the Trinidadian population.

Class

A crisp, discrete definition of class is impossible. The indices which are used to parcel out a population into classes are so numerous as to include most socially distinguishing features—income, occupation, family background, religious orientation, schooling, speech, behavior, associations, personal appearance, type of residence, locale of residence and so forth. A constellation of several of these features may be used to denote membership in a social category, and one can refer to a recurrence of such constellations among a population as indicative of wider social categories we may call classes. *Class* is a broad concept then, broader than any of the particular items (i.e., income) used to index it. The concept "class" embodies the interplay of various sociocultural features as these emerge from the conditions of adaptation. Members of a class develop an outlook, a conception of reality, of "is" and "ought." In defining classes, we seek to locate patterns of behavior or ideology and to construct from these an ideal model of class configuration. Locating such patterns is a frustrating task as the particular indices of class membership, embodied in personal style and presentation, shift as a person presents different facets of his social persona at various occasions, and as such facets are judged differentially.

I may, for example, see someone on a Port-of-Spain street whose class position I want to ascertain. I make an initial guess, forming a gestalt out of the significant items I notice. Wanting to learn more, I seek to identify what this person's various conceptions of his own status are, how other people judge his position, how his class *image* changes with the situation. There is often a sharp contrast between a person's class *origins* and his class *appearance.* A person may conceal his class origins; he may manipulate his class appearance. Appearance is a shifting, changing quality, particularly because the meaning of class varies among different social aggregates in a society. For some, someone designated as "low-class" is to be embraced as a brother; for others he is spurned as undesirable.

Two decades ago, the designation "lower-class" was almost universally a stigma; but in recent years a large number of Trinidadians, predominantly young, embrace this designation, and contrast it with what are now repudiated defining qualities of other designations, such as "bourgeois." The cultural attributes that previously signaled lower-class status—failure to delay gratification and plan frugally; aloofness from the proprieties of bourgeois hopes; insufficient respect for law and order; exaggerated hedonism—were turned inside out and converted from negative attributes to celebrated themes. Poor young men took bourgeois indictments head-on, reinterpreted them, and in turn indicted bourgeois worldviews and critiques as reflections of oppressive, fossilized attitudes which had stunted Caribbean freedom for centuries.

The material aspects of lower-class conditions—poverty and its residues—are still stigmatizing (witness the rather general contempt accorded Shantytown dwellers), though they too can be celebrated as the consequences of a refusal to turn toward materialist aspirations. Jamaican Rastafarians, to use the most obvious example, have embraced material poverty as a sanctified condition, one which keeps the poor pure in spirit.

But in Trinidad it is the man who consistently exemplifies the best of proletarian culture while at the same time devising means of making a living and thereby escaping from material poverty—the successful hustler, for example—who is often held in highest esteem by many in the ghetto. Some exhibit this respect for a savvy, street-wise style openly; others keep their admiration to themselves, unwilling to applaud deviant styles openly, but privately they admire the man who makes it without giving up his identity to the demands of the middle-class world. Tom Wolfe captured much of what is involved in this ideological transformation when he described lower-class styles of presentation in San Francisco:

> In the ghettos the brothers grew up with their own outlook, their own status system. Near the top of the heap was the pimp style. In all the commission reports, and studies, and syllabuses you won't see anything about the pimp style. And yet there it was. In areas like Hunter's Point boys didn't grow up looking up to the man who had a solid job working for some company or for the city, because there weren't enough people who had such jobs. It seemed that nobody was going to make it *by* working, so the king was the man who made out best by *not* working, and by *not* sitting all day under the man's bitch box. And on the street the king was the pimp. Sixty years ago Thorstein Veblen wrote that at the very bottom of the class system, down below the "working class" and the "honest poor," there was a "spurious aristocracy," a leisure class of bottom dogs devoted to luxury and aristocratic poses (emphases in the original, Wolfe 1970:130).

Although there are fewer aristocratic poseurs in Port-of-Spain, Wolfe's assessment applies very nicely to Trinidad.

Though class is ultimately linked to economic position and, most of all, to income, it is important to distinguish between the essentially economic criteria dividing social strata distinguished from each other, and what may be called class culture. Since people faced with similar economic conditions are likely to form a community of a sort (although this "community" need not be based on proximate residence), cultural forms develop around divisions that are basically economic in nature, reflecting in their design specific adaptive concerns. But these cultural forms are never merely a gross reflection of the economic aspects of these adaptations. They have their own dynamics.

In Port-of-Spain the poor are overwhelmingly black (Trinidad's rural poor, by contrast, are overwhelmingly East Indian). Available occupations include work in industry and construction, taxi driving, odd jobs with commercial firms, hotel and domestic work, municipal employment such as road maintenance and street cleaning. Some occupations allow ghetto people to earn rather good incomes by using skills that are especially well developed in the lower-class community—occupations such as used car sales and other legitimate sorts of work that make use of the same skills and dispositions that go into hustling. But earnings alone are not the sole determinant of class position. The contrast between blue- and white-collar work is very marked in Trinidad. Many blacks scorn anything but white-collar office and sales jobs. This partly reflects the proletarian basis of the slave experience and points to a continuing disdain for manual labor by a sector for whom such work signifies a history of extreme oppression. There is marked sensitivity among blacks to the appearance of a job. Since jobs are related to class status, job seekers attempt to secure those sorts of positions which on the surface look good to other people. Hence a job in a modern, air-conditioned office which allows an employee to wear a white shirt is often preferred to what may be a far better and more highly paid job which has a less prestigious ambience. The signs of a position tend to be very conspicuously displayed. A knowledgeable civil servant with whom I often spoke about such matters had this to say regarding the importance of prestige in the selection of work among middle-class "colored" men:

> You know all the middle-class people—the "colored" middle-class
> that is—who would go into the professions almost always chose law
> or medicine. You often hear that until recently these were *the* two
> professions and that other professions hadn't opened up yet. But
> that's not the whole story. Middle-class people who became doctors
> always wore three piece suits, and relished doing so, and had offices
> in Woodbrook. They really looked the part. Anyone seeing them
> would immediately say "doctor" or "attorney." Their status was
> apparent to everyone. But take a petroleum engineer or an agrono-
> mist. He would come into Port-of-Spain from the fields on a Friday
> wearing a khaki shirt, khaki shorts, khaki socks—dirty and tired
> from working in the country. People would look at him and figure
> him to be an ordinary laborer. So people were thinking "What's
> the point of going into a profession that wouldn't make my status
> clear to those who came upon me?" Medicine, law, and three-piece
> suits—that was the answer. That's why West Indian doctors and
> attorneys are all over Africa but when we need engineers, as we do
> now, we have to bring them down from the U.S. or Canada.

An expanded concept of class, which includes cultural themes, and not merely economic position, approaches what Weber called a "status group." For Weber, "status" points not simply to a slot in a hierarchy of positions but to the total *class situation*. Status groups are not identified solely by economic indices, but by lifestyles. Purely economic conceptions of class are too simplistic, and although in recent decades analytical emphasis has shifted away from cultural aspects, narrowly Marxist and economically deterministic notions of class are continually contradicted by the events of this world.

Identifying a status group, discretely defining a lifestyle and the persons who evoke it, is often quite difficult, especially in a complex setting such as Port-of-Spain. To illuminate Trinidadian class concerns one has to look not to categories, but to individuals who in their shifting concerns and commitments embody the multiple facets of lifestyles. People move back and forth in their attachment to various styles as their interests and circumstances change. That is why I have chosen to focus much of the description on particular people and events rather than seeking to identify, and to homogenize, groups whose reality is evanescent.

Ethnicity

> The Negroes are bad people. You musnt't ever let them too near
> you. They're rowdy and rude you know, and they use foul language.
> If you say something to one of them, they tell you to shut your
> mouth. You simply must ignore them.
>
> > (a nine year old "colored," middle-class girl)

> You look at me. No one in Trinidad would say I was Negro. And
> I never thought of myself as that. But then I look at your American
> magazines and I see this fellow Julian Bond who is supposed to be
> a Black Power politician and he is lighter, and looks more like a
> white man than me.
>
> > (a "colored" civil servant)

From the point of view of most Trinidadians, ethnic affiliation is the key criterion in determining a person's membership in socially significant groups. Trinidad is a remarkably polyethnic society and nowhere is this more apparent than in Port-of-Spain. Socioeconomic position joins ethnicity in establishing parameters for social action. Like class, ethnicity eludes precise definition. For the purposes of making some sense of the Trinidadian social ambience, ethnicity may be said to refer to distinctions people make among each other on the basis of physical phenotype, and the cultural styles these phenotypic representations come to symbolize. These styles include, besides organizational features, such markers as speech, dress, cuisine, esthetic preferences, modes of somatic and kinetic presentation and so forth.

The making of ethnic distinctions is an enthusiastic concern of most Trinidadians. Though people living in ethnically homogeneous regions of the country are well aware of Trinidad's polyethnic character, it is in Port-of-Spain and the other large towns where ethnic styles are directly available for scrutiny, and where ethnicity takes on an especially salient dimension as people continually run into others who are different from themselves. Here stereotypes are matched against experience and new assessments (including new stereotypes) emerge.

There are two important questions here. What are the relevant factors in phenotypic identification and how does this identification affect a person's placement of the self and of others? What are the links connecting ethnicity, class structure and national character; that is, what is black and what is lower class and what is Trinidadian about black, lower-class, Trinidadians?

In Trinidad the emergence of a recognizable category of *"colored"* persons has been especially important in the development of a national ethnic mosaic. This importance has its origins in the preferential treatment accorded to mulatto children by their white fathers during and after slavery. What emerged was a distinct group of "coloreds" who remained under the power and control of the white elite, but who themselves became an elite of a sort in contrast to blacks. With the preferential treatment accorded them, "coloreds" consolidated power and influence in certain areas of Trinidadian life, particularly in staffing professional positions and the civil service. To this day the "colored" sector has consistently sought to differentiate itself as much as possible from other Afro-Americans, identifying itself closely with the white elite and sharing that elite's contempt for blacks. But the position of "coloreds" in Trinidad has always been tenuous. They clearly had rights, privileges and powers which differentiated them from blacks, but just as clearly they stood several steps behind the white elite. Such differentiation continues to prevail today, and in most Caribbean societies light-skinned blacks continue to lord it over the darker masses while they are still excluded from the guarded circles of white Creoles and foreigners.

The "colored" middle-class, then, tends to be drawn to white cosmopolitan styles and repelled by indigenous black culture. But ambiguities remain and throughout Trinidadian history, particularly in recent years, many "coloreds" have come to understand this. There have always been members of the "colored" middle-class who were clearly aware and proud of their African origins. As men of some power and influence within the colony, these reformist "colored" professionals were early defenders of black and proletarian rights. During the 1920s and 1930s, many became committed to socialist and anti-imperialist goals, turning their attention and loyalties to the black lower classes, and away from an increasingly repudiated white elite.

Recently, with the emergence of black power politics and the growing recognition that many leading advocates of black rights in the United States—including the more militant—were, from a Trinidadian point of view, clearly "colored," young "colored" men and women have repudiated their special status more and more as they have begun to see themselves as being black. But many "coloreds" find themselves walking a delicate ethnic tightrope; they sometimes manage to walk the rope with finesse, and sometimes fall as they miscalculate the congruence between their own ethnic self-conceptualizations and the definitions accorded them by finger-pointing outsiders. Such definitions shift with circumstances as differing ascriptions and self-descriptions emerge. Ethnic attributions, because phenotype cues are not enough, often become matters for negotiation, maneuver and deception.

Ethnicity is not a feature to parcel people out into fixed categories; it is an active process that enlivens strategic interchanges of all sorts.

One sees a man on the street and tentatively designates him as "colored." But it is not phenotypic features per se that are the diacritic keys to this assessment; one must also guess about his genealogy and current social position by scrutinizing personal display and tacitly assembling various cues into an image that becomes an assessment of the other's inclusion in a particular social category. In the case of this hypothetical "colored" man encountered on the street, there are several possible ways to reconstitute his background and make a guess about his current social status. Consider two such possibilities.

Both the man's parents or even all four of his grandparents may have been "colored." He is then likely to define himself—and to be defined—as a member of an ethnic group which regards itself as a discrete sector among others. Most members of the "colored" middle-class tend to have this sort of background. I knew many such men, but let's call this hypothetical character "Winston." Another man may have one white or very light-skinned parent, and another very dark or black one. Let's call this man "Trevor." In regard to phenotypic categories, Winston and Trevor are indistinguishable from each other. But because their social backgrounds and positions are likely to be different, and because they exhibit signs of such differences, they will tend to be subject to very distinct sorts of ascriptions. On the other hand, their phenotypic resemblance and the ambiguity of categorization such resemblance feeds, makes ethnic presentation often a negotiable matter.

Trevor, the offspring of a union between a light parent (usually the father) and a dark one (typically the mother) is likely to take a rather different path through life than Winston. The chances are good that his conception resulted from a casual liaison. The half of Trevor's kin on his mother's side, whom he is likely to know most intimately, are darker than he is. He may have a darker half-sibling as a result of his mother's unions with other men. In short, Trevor is far more likely to occupy a black social landscape than a "colored" one. Through all this he may or may not come to think of himself as being "black." He may realize that there are advantages to be gained from playing up the fact that he is light-skinned, as he sees those darker than himself being accorded worse treatment. He may notice that he is rarely bothered or scrutinized when he walks through a middle-residential enclave while boys darker than he are regularly harassed by the police and the ever vigilant bourgeoisie on the lookout for troublesome outsiders. He becomes aware that better jobs, such as bank clerkships, are typically filled by light-skinned men and women, and only rarely by darker Afro-Americans. He may be treated better by his mother and other kinsmen than are his darker half-siblings because of his favored skin color. Yet he is likely to grow up in a black, proletarian social milieu and most of his associations are with people darker than himself. He soon realizes that though he may be light-skinned, he is not treated as an equal by "colored," middle-class children who, reading various cues, become aware of his proletarian background. The social characterization of ethnic membership, he learns, depends on much more than just skin color and other physical features. Whites and those from the "colored" middle-class may disparage him as a "low-class nigger;" blacks may view him as "light" and somewhat different and distant from themselves. This shifting topography of ethnic ascription varies with different occasions and settings as Trevor is continually scrutinized, while making ad hoc decisions regarding how to present himself to others—how he wishes to "come off."

The classificatory mechanisms of ethnic attribution are variably activated as the scenes wherein ascriptions are made change. Trevor may be living in limbo as the slippery inconsistencies of treatment accorded him in various situations call into question any regular, working notion of what sort of person he is, ethnically speaking. Or he may approach such ambiguity as a resource and maneuver it with skill and finesse, anticipating what sorts of presentations are most likely to bring about the best pay-offs in varying circumstances. Trevor may be one of the "brothers" in Belmont, but when he heads out toward suburban social scenes with a middle-class ambience he may invoke all those postures that make passing into a bourgeois world possible. If he is skillful and keeps his cool, he may be able to approach all sorts of settings that are closed to his darker brothers. But those who control such settings are always on the lookout for intrusive outsiders, and so he takes risks and faces the possibility of rejection. He may find that he has access to women who wouldn't take a second look at a darker man, and such expanded opportunities may dazzle him. But the recognition of this advantage is apt to irk his darker peers. They may contemptuously remind him that he is not behaving like what he is—a black man—but instead acting like a limbo-living social climber seduced by the temptations of "light fruit" and masquerading in a fragile universe of ethnic hypocrisy. Ethnicity may be negotiable, but at other times it demands commitment.

There are a vast number of possible scenarios and a vast number of possible outcomes as Trevor meanders around what, for him, is a treacherous Trinidadian social world, attempting to mediate his own definition of self to his own advantage. And he can always slip up, as he loses hold of these definitions and fails to recognize what sorts of positions are advantageous. This fluid and slippery landscape is characteristic of polyethnic societies as assorted framing strategies are invoked with rapidly changing and shifting circumstances.

Our hypothetical Winston also occupies this landscape, and although his social trajectories are apt to be quite different from Trevor's, he faces similar contingencies as a negotiator of his variously presented persona. The chances are good that, throughout his childhood as a "colored" bourgeois, he has learned to keep his contempt for the darker riffraff with whom he shares a genealogical heritage alive. In the past there has been little emphasis on the links joining West Indians of African descent; rather, people have tended to dwell on the differences, often mere phenotypic nuances, that separate and alienate. Among younger "colored" men and women such attitudes have changed considerably in recent years. If Winston should happen to be a university student, he likely rejects the special badge of privilege that being colored could otherwise provide, and he desires to seek a new rapport with what he now views as his black brothers and sisters. While he may return home to a middle-class suburb where such uncertainties are rarely voiced, in other contexts he seeks and sometimes gains affiliation to the poor, black people with whom he feels he shares a background. But he may face resistance as well, and be viewed with distrust, or at least ambivalence, by those who are not quite ready to let the barriers down, recognizing as they do the cool and often hostile distance "coloreds" have so vigorously attempted to keep from the black masses in the past, as several unfortunate "Winstons" I knew were pained to discover. At other times, laying his ideological commitments aside for the moment, he may easily reinvoke his notion of himself as "colored" while attending a solidly bourgeois event from which he knows his otherwise brothers-in-struggle are apt to be excluded.

Trevor and Winston may be aware of these inconsistences or they may not. They may aim for consistency and an articulated and cohesive sense of self; or they may move through various scenes like chameleons on the lookout for advantage, always ready to pull one or another mask out of their repertory of presentations. And often they blunder, unable to convey a satisfactory and convincing sense of self to others.

Ethnic designation involves the active use of cultural signifiers, or clusters of symbols, which serve as vehicles for marking a person's (or groups's) social style and position. These signifiers draw on historically established repertories of attributes which contrast with the repertories of other categories of membership—normative, stylistic and phenotypic features including skin color and other indices of appearance; speech and other expressive styles; markers of social position and background; esthetic tastes and so forth. Such features may be the bases of outsiders' indictments, but they can also serve as resources that the ethnically ambiguous actor may attempt to manipulate to his own advantage.

Although my focus has been on those who, ethnically and socially, are black and poor, I have turned attention here to the situation of light-skinned Afro-Americans because such a focus is especially apt to reveal the general mechanisms of ethnic designation and maneuver in a society such as Trinidad. Ethnicity, like class, has been a key factor in the development of styles of social stratification in Trinidad. Ethnic groups in present-day Trinidad have clear cultural and national roots that originated beyond the island, and although such original roots have been markedly altered in the course of the New World experience and a widely pervasive creolization has set in as well, these connections are still strong, and generally acknowledged by those whose definition of self they affect. This generalization is clearly true of such relatively recent migrants as the East Indians, but it is true for those of African descent as well.

Although by no means homogeneous, Afro-American lifestyles have embodied distinctive themes as blacks have transformed (and have had transformed for them) originally African styles into new amalgams owing much to the characteristic shape of the New World experience. Let us consider some features of these amalgams.

Black cultural life has been distinguished by specific *esthetic preferences.* These include not only widely recognized musical and dance forms, but a preoccupation with esthetics and style in everyday life. While many African institutions and styles were denigrated by elitist cultural, religious, and political powers, esthetic styles largely managed to survive, and eventually to thrive. An esthetic preoccupation is not merely exemplified by the superlative music and dance which has emerged from Afro-American communities, but by the permeation of esthetic concerns through so much of cultural and social life generally. As a population meticulously stripped of its power and social flexibility, black people have shown a special concern for style and appearance in public presentation and the manipulation of social resources. With few concrete, conventional advantages to marshall for maximizing opportunity, blacks have come to rely heavily on the importance of appearances in social life. Such reliance has been repeatedly criticized by the bourgeoisie who look upon blacks as displaying excessive concern with the accoutrements of appearance, such as a dazzling wardrobe. But blacks have learned the importance of controlling the impact of esthetic display in gaining advantage. This concern is particularly striking in urban settings where competition for resources leads to a strong emphasis on stylistic care in personal presentation, since such care promises concrete pay-offs.

Unlike other ethnic groups, who have not been systematically stripped of much of their culture, and who sometimes have successfully managed to hold together what they conceived to be an original and pristine sociocultural cohesiveness, blacks have become cynical about social and cultural conformity, particularly when it entails adherence to designs not of their own making. The emergence of *cynicism* as a distinctive outlook toward social life should not be surprising when one considers the history of harassment, disappointment, thwarted expectations, and social impotence characteristic of black social life in Trinidad since the introduction of slavery. It is difficult to portray the tone such cynicism adopts, but it amounts to a skeptical, often sarcastic and sometimes bitter, and yet usually gentle and mellow posture in public behavior, especially in speech and song. The lyrics of almost any Calypso reflect this style (as do other black musical forms such as Jamaican reggae, and American blues). This is a distinctly Afro-American cultural focus, with origins in the unique history of black slavery and oppression. It is never entirely fatalistic, and is only deceptively resigned. Beneath a surface of composure, a seething "don't tread on me" anger lurks. This style reflects the enormous capacity to endure difficult circumstances, but also an insistence on taking critical stands. It is an informed and realistic cynicism.

Individualism is a more distinctive cultural value for blacks than for any other ethnic segment in Trinidad. This, again, results from the slave experience and the resultant socioeconomic disorder and decay which followed. A long tradition holds that the consequences of such disorder led to an extreme disintegration of Afro-American community life, and to a social atomism that left blacks without supportive social networks. This is not true. What is true is that Afro-American social organization is not built around discreet groups (such as kin) which prescribe roles and statuses for members; instead blacks have adopted a looser, more adaptable organizing mode that centers on ad hoc social liaisons as these seem useful and appropriate. Hence the security and continuity made possible by belonging to fixed groups is replaced by a greater focus on individual resiliency. This involves developing the social savvy that permits one to make more good guesses than bad ones in regard to what sorts of social links will prove useful and supportive, a tendency considerably more apparent in an urban than a rural context. The less rigidly fixed social organization is—and Afro-American social organizaton tends to be far less rigid than others—the more freedom people have to make personal choices which are attuned to their circumstances. But the corollary here is that, in poverty, it becomes *more necessary* for persons to use personal freedom strategically, since they may have little else to lean on.

Ethnic styles arise out of particular conditions and adaptations; continuing emphasis on such styles presupposes a stable social milieu. That is, although ethnic culture is a repository of ideas and outlooks that have taken on distinctive parochial forms—forms ideologically flavored and intergenerationally transmitted—these have developed largely as outcomes of class relations and continue to be directly linked to class conditions. For those blacks whose social views become increasingly bourgeois, commitment to ethnic culture wanes as this culture no longer provides an important grounding. In Trinidad, to some extent at least, the durability of ethnic cultural styles requires the continuation of the sort of social conditions which originally gave rise to those styles. As poor, ethnically distinguishable persons become more mobile and find their social positions changing, their attachment to ethnic cultural styles is modified as they turn to cosmopolitan bourgeois culture for new cues. For many of the poor, such a shift on the part of their more successful brothers and sisters represents cultural treason.

Men, Women and Households

Social research in Afro-American communities has stressed the finding that by failing at work and breadwinning, a man fails at masculinity (Liebow 1967). This finding supports the assumption, curiously widespread, that the most important male function is providing for women and families, and that all men aspire to fulfill this function as a prerequisite for full masculine status. Since so many lower-class men fail as providers, the argument goes, they are unable to assert masculinity in this fashion. Instead they turn to other modes of invoking masculinity—physical toughness, sexual appeal and so forth. These other modes are seen not so much as achievements in themselves, but as reflections of a failure to perform adequately in the bread-winning mode. They are second-best alternatives. To the extent that those in the lower-class community adopt a middle-class work ethic and view failure in actualizing this ethic through concrete achievements as corroding their masculine integrity, this claim may be true. But in Trinidad, among the poor, black men I have been describing, this ethic is only partially accepted, and frequently spurned.

Peter Wilson has made a useful distinction between two different moral orientations of poor, black Caribbean men. One of these he calls "reputation," the underlying rationale behind the presentations of younger men. The other he refers to as "respectability," which becomes a compelling concern behind behavioral choices among older men (Wilson 1969). Prestige accrues to younger men according to the image they are able to present of themselves as winners—as manipulators and opportunists, as persons who know how to make the most of things and are able to convey this impression of themselves to others. As a man grows older, Wilson argues, this source of prestige wanes in importance. He now finds it difficult to compete with younger men who are better equipped to engage in behavior that enhances reputation (seducing women, winning fights, enduring various difficulties with a show of coolness). Furthermore, older men feel increasing pressure to settle down and seek satisfaction by conforming to social rules that prescribe how a mature man should behave and what he should value. Whereas reputation is gauged against codes of conduct which arise out of lower-class conditions, respectability requires conforming to mainstream codes. With a shift from one moral code to another, as respectability takes over from reputation, what once may have been something to take pride in, becomes something to be ashamed of.

In Trinidad women *do* have expectations that men will be supportive providers, but these expectations reflect hope and desire more than any realistic conviction that men will in fact behave in this way. Men do acknowledge that they should fulfill commitments to women and households, but they hold this opinion without much conviction: men tend to remain untroubled by what they know others think of as their failure to perform the roles expected of those who are "responsible." While they know that mainstream society has its definitions of responsible behavior, they themselves are not in direct contact with such standards and are largely immune to external criticism. Instead they share narrower and, for them, more practical ideas regarding the costs of their commitment to women and households.

Most of the men I knew tended to regard women as sexual objects and little more. Although these men proclaimed great love and respect for mothers (often called "queens," while no father would ever be referred to as "king"), wives and lovers tended to be mere "chicks"—women to be exploited for their sexual availability, their services, and sometimes for their money. Men were especially troubled by what they called "social" women— those with middle-class pretensions who made excessive demands of men and who tended to spurn those who were too poor or too dark. This kind of woman is a constant thorn for men who do not expect women to remain aloof from them on principle. Pursuing such a "social chick" successfully becomes a small triumph, as the pursuer basks in the glory of what he considers his ultimately irresistible charm, seducing a woman who presented herself as inaccessible to a "sort" like him. Men are unwilling to make sacrifices and to work out problems with women; it is too easy to walk away from problems and go searching for new women. Women know this and fortify themselves with a resiliency and resignation attuned to the unreliability of men.

It has been repeatedly claimed that Caribbean women enjoy a great deal of freedom and power in their relations with men. But this freedom and power are necessary armaments in a world where women can depend only irregularly on men as committed partners in managing life's mundane concerns. Women find they must be strong and rely on kin to insure the cooperation necessary in managing households successfully and in raising families in poverty. Men, greedy for their freedom and aloof in their relationships with women, are hardly then in a position to enforce women's behavior and movements as they so often are in other societies. Nevertheless, the Caribbean woman's freedom is illusory. Women become entangled in the difficulties and responsibilities of raising children and supporting stable households. Men, with fewer responsibilities, are freer in their social movements. The argument that men feel emasculated by their inability to head families, while no doubt true elsewhere, hardly applies in Trinidad. Black Trinidadian men tend to be self-pleased strutters. They are less abusive and authoritarian toward women than are men in many other societies, and consequently Trinidadian women are freer from abuse, but men are in no position to even seek to be enforcers.

The Trinidadian man's approach to women tends first and foremost to be manipulative; after that it is contemptuous. Though men seek their sexual services, and though they "make babies," women have little to do with the core of meaningful experience as most men see it. Men feel that women should not hinder their independence, although they realize that women can make things difficult for them. Therefore women must be fooled and cajoled; and it is better to be subtle in one's deception than to be brazenly arrogant and abusive. Men are admired for a show of "cool" in handling women—getting their way without nakedly exerting power and authority. Those who exhibit a "don't take any shit" attitude, typified by exercising authority and will through command and force, tend to be less successful, and other men evaluate their strategy as less effective and far less graceful than more indirect and wily maneuvers. Furthermore, men who assume force to gain power with women often find that they can back it up with very little clout, having nothing they can really withdraw from women and few effective threats. Women are generally able to escape male tyranny since there are few sanctions supporting such domination and many escape routes to comforting and protective others.[11]

Women often resent what they consider the intrusion of their men's unacceptable activities and acquaintances upon their households. Men like to brush this resentment aside, and claim that though this and that man has a woman who puts humiliating pressure on him, they themselves have control over their women. There is much braggadocio here, but the boasting is often very hesitant. Although women generally have little influence over men's actions, they do manage to retain significant control over what goes on in their homes, and this is one reason that men prefer to carve out social worlds for themselves away from their homes. Whereas male identity has little to do with effectiveness in the household, female success and identity is structuraly linked to it. It is in the household, and often only there, that a woman may feel a sense of permanence and control in the design of her life. However tenuous her relationship with men may be, household links between mothers and children, and mothers and female relatives and friends tend to be solid. It means very little for a man to be "head" of a household. Since a household is an arena for female concerns, to be its head is really a hollow position of authority for a man.

Typically children are raised by their mothers and maternal relatives. Often a father is not present in the house, and sometimes a child lives in an essentially fatherless world. In such matrifocal household settings, fathers tend to be absent or only irregularly present, and mother-child relations become the core of family life and household socialization. Scholars have often claimed that under such conditions sentimental bonds between mothers and children are very strong, perhaps reflected in the designation of the mother as "queen" in the talk of Trinidadian men. This is sometimes true, but absence of a father may also create strain, as a mother may begin to feel that a child is an unwanted reminder of a best to be forgotten relationship, a bitter reminder of failure and fiasco in an episode with a man.

While elsewhere in this book I have stressed the integrity shown by black, proletarian men in the face of difficult and challenging circumstances, in the domain of male-female relationships men tend to show little such integrity. The same man who takes a stand on behalf of those who are black and poor—who shows moral courage—displays moral corruption in his behavior toward women. Here male identity and prerogatives transcend ethnic compassion and solidarity. The flippant behavior of men towards women has been explained away by pointing to a vast array of causal factors, but these explanations do not erase the clear recognition that men so often tend to treat women contemptibly. To witness the Trinidadian man's typical attitudes and actions toward women is to observe what, together with the abuses generated by economic greed and rapacious lust for status at the expense of others, is most ugly in Trinidadian life.

Chapter 5

Assessments

Over the past two decades anthropological notions of culture have become increasingly complex and, so it seems to me, rarefied. Anthropologists have described culture as sets of discrete rules, systems of symbols, models and structures, circuits of communication. They have variously located culture in the spaces *between* people and spaces *within* the brain. They have seen culture as analogous with mind, logic, language, ecology, artifact. But none of this has really improved on that most useful and sensible view of cultures as *styles* of life, as *designs* for living. To the systematizing scientist ("culturologist") this rather loose and seemingly evasive view of culture as style or design seems vague and unsatisfying. It doesn't appear quite crisp enough—where is its elegance, its parsimony? Such a view does not permit the tinker-toy manipulations which in recent years have so charmed anthropologists. This rather easy definition of culture as lifestyle does not provide options for technical forms of analysis. Sly Stone, that maverick and inventive soul singer and composer, popularized a view of culture as "different strokes for different folks," an attitude that makes sense to me. The interesting question is then: how did these strokes come about, and how comfortable are different folks with their different strokes—how do they "wear" them? These are the sorts of questions Boas, Lowie, Mead, Kluckhohn, Redfield, Evans-Pritchard and Geertz have asked. And they are still very good questions, despite the criticism of such unoperational views leveled by more "modern" and "precise" articulators of a concept of culture.

There is a newly popular epistemology in the social sciences (and especially in anthropology, which in recent years has been in quest of precision) propounding a compelling—and compulsive—intellectual need to grip aspects of reality as clearly delineated *somethings* which, once identified, can be transformed into crystalline models; pulverized and quantized into numbers: or dissected into neat, rearrangable pieces. These modes of thinking, mechanistic in their assumptions, have their sources in a Newtonian-Cartesian worldview whose underlying operations are analytical and structural. This style of thought has been immensely productive in illuminating much about the organization of physical reality. Applied to *life,* and particularly to human life, proponents of this view search for the underlying processes and rules of arrangement which they assume to lie under the apparent shapelessness of everyday surfaces. In some domains of inquiry, molecular biology and linguistics, for example, such an outlook has been successful. But for other domains, such as those of human culture and experience, the optimism of the analytical approach is unwarranted, and is continually shattered by the vagaries of experience. The reality of history challenges any analytical optimism which assumes that we can understand human experience in terms of a few basic principles and the operations generated by them; Levi-Strauss is the most notorious exponent of such a distorted epistemology. Such a view to one extent or another, propels the thinking of American ethnoscientists, French structuralists, and structure-crazed Marxists.

The idea of *style,* in contrast, acknowledges the paramount reality of history. Style is embodied in the progression of events, the collections of moments comprising the life of a person or a society or an era. Style is the tone or texture of these interconnected events and moments. And consequently we must look for culture *in* history, not outside of it.

While historical experience, mediated by the mind, is transformed into cultural outlooks, one cannot claim, as does Levi-Strauss, that such outlooks are homologues of these mental mediations. The structuralists search for underlying regularities beneath a surface of variations. But, one may ask, why seek to do this? Or, in fact, is such a quest really possible?

Partly all this becomes a matter of taste rather than logic. I am quite comfortable with looking upon a cultural ambience, such as that of Trinidad, and seeing it as a morass of interwoven themes; rich, dense and disorderly—like a tropical forest. Much less appealing to me are crisply etched, arid landscapes. I prefer the density of history to the geometry of structure much as I prefer Vermeer to Mondrian. But there are other reasons to be skeptical about the claims of the structuralists, and these concern the differences between describing the principles that shape an entity, and describing the form of the entity itself. We can take a piece of music and analyze it in terms of its constituent elementary structures, but any piece of music is much more than an arrangement of structures—it is the outcome of someone's efforts, located in space and time (c.f. Geertz 1973 for a superb discussion of these matters).

That is, culture is the *product,* and not the mechanism which make the product possible. The study of culture should certainly not exclude such mechanisms, as they range from the broad consistencies and contradictions of social arrangements which Marx illuminated, to the developmental regularities of cognitive development that Piaget has exposed. But identifying ecological processes (ecologies of society *and* of mind) is not the same as interpreting the results of such processes. These concrete products are *events.* Following Geertz, we may regard culture as the results of social interactions as these make use of historically deposited repertories of options put to use within particular social arenas. That is, people always find themselves within some historically established social space; they never find themselves in society "in general." Their ranges of social maneuver are not determined by this space in any simple fashion, but such a range does reflect the social trajectories that have brought people to whatever spaces they happen to occupy. Culture arises and may be observed at specific points of unfolding action, not in the minds of actors. The mind includes cultural representations in the form of competence and memory, but for culture itself we must look in the centers of activity, and not in obscure corners of the mind.

Scanning these arenas of activity can one then claim, as an anthropologist, that some cultural fields are richer, livelier and more inventive than others? On the whole, anthropologists have taken a coolly neutral attitude toward the *evaluation* of culture, and for very good reasons. Against the presumptions of "high culture," ethnographers have pressed convincing claims that culture is a human universal, and that all societies are animated by cultural outlooks that differ from each other but cannot be scaled as "better" or "worse." Anthropologists, it is usually claimed, can really do no more than to illuminate various cultural styles and to regard them comparatively. And this leaves no room for praise and condemnation, simply neutral description.

Certainly the most noble accomplishment of anthropology has been the demolition of the notion that civilization, particularly of the Western sort, is a magnificent and sublime achievement, transcending the "ruder" conditions of less noble folk. Such was the thinking of many of the social evolutionists who founded anthropology as a scholarly discipline in the nineteenth century. With Boas and Malinowski, a fierce relativism began to dominate ethnographic outlooks, and it still does. Among the Northwest Coast Indians and the Trobriand Islanders anthropologists discovered cultures that certainly seemed as rich and complex as any. Kwakiutl art is no less an esthetic accomplishment than Michelangelo's ceiling, the Trobriand kula ring no less an articulated economic mechanism than the balance of trade. But relativism, while certainly on the whole having done its job in dismantling the arrogant claims of Euro-Christian chauvinism, need not go on to deny the possibility that cultures may, in some cases, be assessed as greater or lesser achievements. Let me attempt to defend this heresy by drawing on the Caribbean experience.

In one of his most provocative and condemned statements, Oscar Lewis, describing the culture of the poor in urban Mexico and Puerto Rico, claimed that the culture of poverty includes as one of its very key features a *poverty of culture* (Lewis 1966:Iii). In response, many have argued, quite persuasively at times, that there can be no such thing as a poverty of culture—how can one group be claimed to have "more" or "less" culture than another? What there can be is a poverty of those resources which make possible the achievement of cultural goals. And yet the notion of a poverty of culture may be viewed not as deficiency of magnitude but as a deficiency of quality. And in this regard, Lewis paints a compelling portrait of a social setting whose cultural ambience is narrow and rigid. Some have claimed that this portrait reveals more about Lewis's sour and glum disposition than it does about urban slum dwellers. But Lewis may have been on to something, even if we wish to dispute his descriptions of Mexican and Puerto Rican lifestyles. What he may have grasped is the anthropologist's right to *assess* a culture, and not merely to *describe* it.

What are we to say, for example, of a cultural view that includes as one of its dominant themes the notion that the cool and arbitrary exploitation and enslavement of other peoples is perfectly all right as long as it serves to enhance that culture's greed for goods and power? The European-focused cultural ambience of the Caribbean reflects precisely such an outlook. If culture is the stylistic distillation of historical events and experience, then the cultural styles of the Caribbean may be seen to reflect foremost two ranges of Caribbean experience: economic exploitation (in and out of slavery), and racism. In this book I have been looking at how such ranges of experience have influenced the outlooks of one population segment: those who are impoverished descendents of African slaves. Against this, I have been alluding to those who established and sought to enforce a culture of dominance, what I have been calling a mainstream. There is much irony here. The exponents of white, European culture are telling the people whose ancestors their ancestors *stole* from their homelands all about what is the proper way to live. The descendents of thieves, killers, and exploiters make moral demands of those whose ancestors their ancestors displaced and plundered.

Let us then briefly consider the culture of a mainstream sector whose intellectual line goes back to the glories of the golden days of colonialism and contrast it with the culture of those who have been the pawns and victims of colonialist exploits. If culture includes ranges of styles distilled from the progression of historical moments, then the cultural styles of a Caribbean society such as Trinidad are linked to two exceedingly different lines of descent. One strand ties together the intentions and achievements of those who controlled and operated the island on behalf of their own interests; the other links those who have been the instruments and victims of such operations.

Some of the elements in the cultural background of the first of these strands are: having conceptualized a sector of humanity that was not European or caucasian as a collection of *things,* as objects or commodities to be conveniently used and abused; enslaving that sector and squeezing it for all it was worth; insisting that this sector, now stripped of its power and independence, repudiate its cultural heritage and accept as a model of propriety the beliefs of its owners, exploiters and executioners; and then erecting various barriers to make it difficult for such proprieties to be lived out; while never hesitating to punish deviations from such proprieties. In short, Europeans came to Trinidad with plunder: African slaves. They put these slaves to work and abused them horribly. They told the slaves how they should live, insisting that things European (like Christianity) were wonderful while things African (like dancing) were despicable; and that they had better do things the European way or else. But then they set up all sorts of barriers in the way of those who tried to live up to these new demands, punishing them if they failed or selected other routes. Such is the background of the island's mainstream. This is what a lucky young member of Trinidad's white elite can think about while pondering his heritage.

The second Caribbean social strand links the overwhelming majority of today's population to ancestors brought over forceably as slaves or, later, as contract labor. Here I have been focusing on one of the segments who share this background—those whose African ancestors made their Trinidadian debut as slaves. Taken from their African homelands, treated as commodities, enslaved and put to work on sugar plantations—such was the initial exposure to the New World for these peoples. European masters methodically weakened or destroyed African social bonds; discouraged the continued expression of African cultural themes; imposed their own cultural standards on slaves while heaping contempt on any signs of residual African style; "converted" slaves to Christianity, especially to very convenient "turn thy other cheek" and "seek thy reward in heaven" sorts of Christian themes, while outlawing or otherwise making difficult the perseverance of African religious beliefs and rituals. They invoked racist ideologies to belittle Africans, thereby justifying their continued subjugation and abuse. Blacks found themselves ridiculed, their ancestral cultures mocked, while at the same time they were expected to adhere to new and foreign standards which seemed, and continue to seem, most striking in their brazen hypocrisy. Caught in this web of contradictions, blacks were continually victimized in all sorts of new and imaginative ways—the oppressor knew no bounds in conceiving of ways to limit the flexibility and freedom of the subordinate population. Afro-Americans have been blamed for being black, for being poor, for not being European, for showing continued commitment to Africanisms. Through all this they have survived and they have endured; they have created for themselves, under the most difficult sorts of conditions, distinctive patterns of adaptation and response. They have sought, and to a large extent they have succeeded, to maintain dignity and integrity. Immensely stoic, resilient, and tough, black Trinidadians have done what they could to preserve and express their commitments and beliefs under conditions designed to erode their strength and independence. This is what a young, poor, black Trinidadian can think about while pondering his heritage, and especially in recent years, *this is exactly what blacks have been thinking about.*

Readers may have noticed that I seemed to have been taking sides throughout this book, sneering at the Trinidadian bourgeoisie and its presumptions. I have. The single inescapable fact about the Caribbean is oppression. And it is absolutely clear who have been the oppressors and who have been the oppressed. The irony is that black West Indians—the oppressed—have been vilified, not only by their oppressors, whose self-serving antagoism we can assume, but by social critics who have so often portrayed black people in a pathetically inadequate and distorted manner as being *without* culture, goals, a viable social organization; as *losers* to be pitied or coddled; as a damaged people in need of many remedies. Against such claims I would argue that black people have responded creatively to their immensely difficult circumstances, articulating perspectives and designing plans to give meaning to their situation and to enhance the flexibility of their lives.

The dominant cultural mode (the mainstream) has these as its key features: arrogance, racism, frivolity, intolerance, domination, greed. Against this the Afro-American sector has responded with stoicism, imagination, estheticism, inventiveness, pride, resiliency, patience, compassion. My assessments should be clear by now; I'll leave the reader to make his or her own.

Notes

1. On this see Jacques Monod's *Chance and Necessity* (New York: Vintage, 1972).
2. On the Jamaica Rastafari see Tracy Nicholas and Bill Sparrow, *Rastafari* (New York-Anchor, 1979); Joseph Owens, *Dread: The Rastafarins of Jamaica* (Kingston: Sangster, 1976); Rex Nettleford, *Identity, Race and Protest in Jamaica* (New York: Morrow, 1977).
3. In Trinidad the term "bourgeois" is widely used by poor people to describe the pretensions of those aspiring to middle-class respectability and status.
4. Similar in connotation to "bourgeois," "social" indicates an inappropriate preoccupation with respectability on the part of the poor, who are unlikely to enjoy the rewards of respectability.
5. In recent years an ideology of "youth" has arisen, reflecting a feeling on the part of many young people that there is developing an increasing distance between their critical outlooks and their elders' complacencies.
6. Wilson introduced this term to describe male groups of friends and associates in his study of Providencia (1971).
7. Used in this sense a *ghetto* is a niche tucked away in a yard or alleyway which serves as a center for marijuana distribution and for casual congregation of marijuana smokers.
8. There are categories of outsiders, however, who make it a point to become familiar with insider argot. Policemen need to familiarize themselves with criminal argot, social workers try to become comfortable with the special street argot of juvenile gang members, and anthropologists are forever attempting to penetrate insider argot, as when they wish to understand secret ritual ceremonies and so forth. But these outsiders can rarely keep up with changes argots undergo as terms and references disappear and are replaced by others. For example, traders can identify an outsider by his outdated or inappropriate use of terms—when they say "weed" and he says "pot"—and this ability to detect semantic nuances serves as an important protective device.
9. An excellent discussion of various modes of resistance on the part of different sorts of American proletariats to the "protestant ethic and the spirit of capitalism" is provided by Herbert Gutman in his "Work,

Culture and Society in Industrializing America," *American Historical Review* 78 (1973).

10. When I was first in Trinidad, these tended to be action films of the "B" sort, usually by such outstanding directors as Howard Hawks, Raoul Walsh and Don Siegel, and starring such perennial Trinidadian favorites as Richard Widmark, Joseph Cotten and James Cagney. In recent years these films have been almost entirely replaced by Kung Fu movies marking a degeneration of Trinidadian film offerings.

11. This is certainly not true of East Indians, for example. Indian men have extensive control over women and their commands are enforceable. Indian women are expected to put on a proper show of servility before men, and men make sure they do, using physical force if they deem it necessary. Except in extreme cases, abused women really have nowhere to run to and nowhere to hide, as their husbands' authority is sanctioned by the community.

References

Bateson, Gregory. *Steps to an Ecology of Mind*. New York: Ballantine, 1972.

Chomsky, Noam. *Language and Mind*. New York: Harcourt, Brace and World, 1968.

_____. *Reflections on Language*. New York: Pantheon, 1975.

Finestone, Herbert, "Cats, Kicks, and Color" in *The Other Side*, ed. Howard Becker. New York: Free Press, 1964.

Geertz, Clifford. "Thick Description," in *The Interpretation of Cultures*. New York: Basic Books, 1973.

Goffman, Erving. *The Presentation of Self in Everyday Life*. New York: Doubleday, 1959.

_____. *Interaction Ritual*. New York: Doubleday, 1967.

_____. *Frame Analysis*. New York: Harper and Row, 1974.

Horton, John. "Time and Cool People" *Transaction* 4 (1967) 5:5-12.

Leach, Edmund. *Rethinking Anthropology*. London School of Economics Monographs on Social Anthropology 22 (1962).

Lewis, Oscar. "The Culture of Poverty" *Scientific American* 215 (1966) 4:19-25.

Liebow, Elliot. *Tally's Corner*. Boston: Little-Brown, 1967.

Lowenthal, David. "Race and Color in the West Indies" *Daedalus* 96 (1967) 2:580-626.

Lynch, Kevin. *The Image of the City*. Cambridge: M.I.T., 1960.

Mangin, William. "Latin American Squatter Settlements: A Problem and a Solution," *Latin American Resarch Review* (1967) 2:65-97.

Polsky, Ned. *Hustlers, Beats and Others*. Chicago: Aldine, 1967.

Rodman, Hyman. *Lower-Class Families: The Culture of Poverty in Negro Trinidad*. New York: Oxford, 1971.

Smith, Raymond. *The Negro Family in British Guiana*. Lond, 1956.

Suttles, Gerald. *The Social Order of the Slum*. Chicago: University of Chicago Press, 1968.

Wilson, Peter. "Reputation and Respectability: A Suggestion for Caribbean Ethnography," *Man* 4 (1969) 1:70-84.

Wilson, Peter. "Caribbean Crews: Peer Groups and Male Society," *Caribbean Studies* 10 (1971) :18-34.

Wolfe, Tom. *Radical Chic and Mau-Mauing the Flak Catchers*. New York: Farrar, Strauss, and Giroux (1970).